LIFE IN THE CONSULTING ROOM

Life in the Consulting Room offers a series of noteworthy vignettes that occurred in the author's consulting room. Although the context and objective of each consultation varied, the decision to present them here is due to a particularly interesting feature of the patient's life or a significant point that arose during their interview with the author. Many of the cases have issues of academic interest but these are not pursued here. Instead, these accounts should be seen as portraits, "snapshots" that were considered emotionally interesting and intellectually stimulating. Some of these patients were in short- or long-term therapy, but most cases were being assessed to determine whether psychotherapy was in fact the best way of helping them. No doubt all psychodynamic practitioners will have met some of these findings in their practice, but the present book offers a particularly significant collection of clinical episodes.

A. H. Brafman trained as a psychoanalyst of adults and children. In his NHS career he worked as a consultant in child and adolescent psychiatry, and for many years ran a group for parents and under-fives. He ran infant observation courses at the Institute of Psychoanalysis and also seminars on psychodynamic work with children, adolescents, and adults for the British Psychoanalytic Society and several other training organisations.

"From his life's work in psychiatry, child psychiatry and psychoanalysis, Dr Brafman has selected some clinical 'Portraits', moments in consultations or treatments when something happened that struck him as a significant communication. He demonstrates how an open mind, patient curiosity, the capacity to bear 'not knowing', together with a deep understanding of psychological development, have allowed him to respond to requests for help that may not be clearly articulated or even understood by the person consulting him. He makes clear that understanding a painful situation can be helpful in itself, and Dr Brafman's own humanity and capacity to do exactly that lays the foundation for interventions that are sometimes surprising, always meaningful. A fascinating book."

Dr Jennifer Johns, Psychoanalyst and Fellow, British Psychoanalytical Society and The Institute of Psychoanalysis.

LIFE IN THE CONSULTING ROOM

Portraits

A. H. Brafman

LONDON AND NEW YORK

First published 2018
by Routledge
2 Park Square, Milton Park, Abingdon, Oxon OX14 4RN

and by Routledge
711 Third Avenue, New York, NY 10017

Routledge is an imprint of the Taylor & Francis Group, an informa business

British Library Cataloguing-in-Publication Data
A catalogue record for this book is available from the British Library

Library of Congress Cataloging-in-Publication Data
A catalog record has been requested for this book

ISBN: 978-1-78220-639-2 (pbk)

Typeset in Palatino LT Std
by Medlar Publishing Solutions Pvt Ltd, India

CONTENTS

ACKNOWLEDGEMENT

I am extremely grateful to my daughter Miriam Speers for her careful, loving, and meticulous help she gave me in the composition of this book.

ABOUT THE AUTHOR

A. H. Brafman trained as a psychoanalyst of adults and children. In his NHS career he worked as a consultant in child and adolescent psychiatry, and for many years ran a group for parents and under-fives. He ran infant observation courses at the Institute of Psychoanalysis and also seminars on psychodynamic work with children, adolescents, and adults for the British Psychoanalytic Society and several other training organisations. He was also honorary lecturer at University College Medical School, where he taught students and psychotherapy trainees. He has published a number of books, including *Untying the Knot, Fostering Independence: Helping and Caring in Psychodynamic Therapies*, and *The Language of Drawings: A New Finding in Psychodynamic Work.*

INTRODUCTION

Life in the consulting room

In recent decades many people have asked what led me to choose psychoanalysis as a profession. I had always enjoyed my work as a physician. Seeing patients with various complaints, I was happy searching for a diagnosis that would enable me to prescribe the medication that might help them to overcome their symptoms. But occasionally I would feel that the patient was also looking for a sympathetic ear, someone with whom she might share emotional problems that she was struggling with. Sadly, my schedule would not allow me to spend much time with each patient. One day I learnt of a new technique, where such a patient was given a longer appointment at the end of the regular daily schedule. Discovering psychoanalysis opened a new door. The "fifty minute hour" allowed time for the patient to voice his pain and it gave me the opportunity to have the emotional closeness that I felt comfortable with. The psychoanalytic training enabled me to achieve the expertise to help people through understanding them.

It was only recently that I recognised that throughout my life I had developed an image of myself as a person willing to be available to whoever approached me seeking help. This was never a choice, but rather an attitude that became part of my personality. It encompassed an endless variety of situations, problems, and challenges, but invariably my attempt to help was a response to a request that was not always explicitly articulated. Some of these people might have tried to obtain help from others, but at times I was told "nobody else knows of this, but I hope you will not mind if I tell you that ..." The moment came when I found myself wondering how I had developed this image and reached this privileged position and this led to the question "why me?" Trying to find an answer, I set out to search examples of this experience and I recovered quite a large number of such situations, involving totally diverse contexts, but the answer still eludes me.

Making presentations of my work with children and their families, and also when a book of mine was being discussed, I have found members of the audience congratulating me for my work, but invariably going on to shake their heads and say, with an apologetic tone of voice, "but ... really ... that is really something that YOU can do ... not for everybody ..." Yes, I have always felt honoured and proud at these words of praise, but that "why me? What is it about me?" question promptly comes to the surface.

My childhood years were spent in unusual circumstances. Out of my maternal grandparents' four children, it was my mother who made a point of living near them and devoted herself to helping them. My cousins lived quite far away from us, so that, being my mother's only son for many years, I was the child who spent time with our grandparents. My grandfather was a teacher, but he led a solitary and unhappy life, with few friends and rare pupils—and I became his "chosen" pupil, spending many hours sitting at his side, following his teaching of Jewish religious texts. My grandmother, much as my mother and all the family knew how much my presence was needed and valued by my "Zeide" (grandfather). It happened that my mother often suffered from health problems and, however loving and devoted my father was to her, he spent long hours working away from home. I have clear memories of spending time in my mother's company following her accounts of personal and family events. I believe that it is these childhood experiences that are the origin of my image of someone willing to listen and, if possible, help the other person, meeting their needs and wishes.

I have no memory of *deciding* to become a doctor. I had worked as a teacher and as a translator and somehow found myself applying to and managing to pass the entrance exams at the National Medical Faculty in Rio de Janeiro, Brazil, in my late teens. After graduating I worked as a general practitioner until deciding to come to London to train at the British Psychoanalytic Society (BPS). This book describes a number of cases I have seen since coming to live in England in 1960. To preserve confidentiality, names have been changed.

I have met a very large number of patients since I became a student at the BPS in 1961. My NHS life started with my working at the Cassel Hospital as a junior doctor. Eventually I became a consultant child and adolescent psychiatrist at Roehampton Child Guidance Clinic and at Queen Mary's Hospital, Roehampton. Once I started my analytic training I began to see private patients and a few yeas after qualification I joined the group of analysts who evaluated applicants for analysis as training cases of students of the Psychoanalytic Society. Soon, other training organisations started to refer applicants to me to assess their suitability to be training cases. Supervising the clinical work of trainees individually or in groups gave me further exposure to the type of people and problems who come to the attention of psychoanalysts and psychotherapists.

For many years I ran weekly supervision meetings of groups of students doing infant observations during the first year of their training at the Institute of Psychoanalysis and the other psychotherapy organisations with which I was associated. I consider this an extremely important element in the growth of my clinical experience. The students visited a mother in the late stages of pregnancy and following the delivery they made weekly visits to observe the characteristics of the development of the baby and of the maternal input. This work has enriched my knowledge of early development and, therefore, influenced the formulation of hypotheses when trying to establish the role of early life in the pathology of patients seen in the consulting room. Another activity that influenced my views on early development was a weekly group meeting that I ran for many years at Roehampton Child Guidance Clinic and Queen Mary's Hospital, Roehampton for children under five years of age, who came to the sessions with their mothers. Sadly, only seldom would the fathers join us.

From the above it is clear that I saw patients in several different contexts. Reading my notes on patients I have seen for a clinical assessment and for short or long-term therapy, as well as checking notes and reports given to me by trainees, I was repeatedly struck by the impact that their words, their feelings, and their life experiences had on me.

Furthermore, it is this rich and complex material that I have decided to share with colleagues and, hopefully, other readers. I will not present a "proper" scientific, academic account. I would rather describe my stories as *portraits*. As mentioned above, working in the consulting room I see myself as a *helper*. I do my best to find a way of helping my patients to achieve insight and relief of their pain. Seeing trainees, my objective is to *help* them to acquire knowledge and to overcome doubts and problems. But outside of my work, I am known as a keen photographer and storyteller (i.e., conveying views in images or words) and it is this particular skill that I am turning to here. I can only hope that my stories/portraits will convey effectively my impressions and that readers may find them equally interesting and revealing.

The stories in the book have been grouped in line with what I thought were their main characteristics. Chapter One "Sex and love" describes relationships where the partners experience and recount attitudes related to sex and love that came across as uncommon and/or surprising. Chapter Two "Unusual solutions" contains cases that came to a completely unexpected resolution; perhaps understandably, once the "solution" is known, it seems quite "obvious", but I do believe that it would have been impossible to guess the outcome of these situations. Chapter Three "Unusual stories" depicts accounts of people finding themselves in circumstances that surprised them and, indeed, came across as unusual and traumatic. Chapter Four "Interesting stories" is a self-explanatory title. Chapter Five "Unusual histories" contains the accounts of people who went through life experiencing relationships and situations that came across as not that common. Chapter Six "Sentences" derives from interviews where someone managed to express a very meaningful sentiment in a succinct, cogent, and impressive few words. Chapter Eight "Intra-vaginal non-ejaculating" describes some men who, whatever their feelings about their sexual partners, were unable to ejaculate when having penetrative sex. Chapter Ten "The replacement child" are some of the cases I have seen where the person had developed a specific pattern of life that I defined as a feeling of *non-entitlement* to success and happiness, which I attributed to their having a sibling who had died before they—my patients—had been born. Finally, I have reproduced some accounts from students' encounters with their patients.

A friend of mine gave me "as a present" the drawing his son had made, depicting how he imagined I looked when seeing my patients.

It was gratifying to find evidence that my work arose this young man's curiosity and interest and I decided to include it here.

Figure 1. Portrait—by Maximilian Travis.

CHAPTER ONE

Sex and love

Some of the following stories came up in diagnostic assessments, others during regular therapy sessions. Only a few of these patients were specifically setting out to discuss their sexual life and what feelings were involved in this. It happens that my fascination with language always leads me to achieve a clear differentiation between wanting and needing, loving and liking, seeking and accepting a finding, attraction and discharge of impulses—sentiments that are usually voiced without much preoccupation as to whether they are conveying a precise rendering of the individual's feelings. It is this "carelessness" that appears in some of the following stories and I can only hope that readers will find them interesting.

Mrs J

I first met Mrs J when her GP referred her son to me. The boy was ten years old and was wetting his bed virtually every night. He overcame this problem after two consultations, but Mrs J contacted me after a few weeks: she needed help with some problems of her own and she believed I might be able to help her. She held a senior position in a bank, and she found herself struggling with crises of anxiety, mostly related to her social life. She told me of her personal history, where I could not pick up any significant factors. After a few interviews, she was able to confide that since the birth of her second child she had lost interest in sex and this meant that she refused to have sex with her husband. We carried on our meetings for several months and Mrs J eventually found that her anxiety crises had disappeared.

Mrs J came to see me again after a few months, to "catch up" with developments. She told me that, at her husband's request, they had been seeing a marital counsellor. Predictably, this led me to ask about her sexual life. "No change ..." she said. I was surprised and asked whether they had discussed this aspect of their married life with the marital counsellor. "Not really ..." And I could not refrain from asking: "But how is this possible?" And she said: "Simple, actually. They never asked about it and we never mentioned it ..."

A couple of years went by and Mr and Mrs J came to see me because one of their sons was presenting behaviour problems. I saw the three of them and then the boy on his own. To round off this series of meetings, I met the couple on their own. Because of the need to maintain confidentiality, I had to find all kinds of "subterfuges" to bring up the issue of sex. When I succeeded, Mr J told me that they had not had any sex since the birth of their younger son. I was able to show my surprise: how had they managed to reach an agreement on this? And I was "put in my place"... Obviously trying not to offend me, Mr J said, "Dr Brafman, there is more to marriage than sex."

Mr A

Mr A sought psychotherapy because of relationship difficulties. He was struggling with his sexual identity and in those days (1980s) this represented a difficult problem. He was a successful architect, now in his mid-thirties, and feeling very unhappy with his solitary life. He felt quite at ease when recounting that as a child he was part of a church choir and that the choirmaster had abused him sexually. Mr A was an only child and both his parents had jobs in a supermarket of the village where they lived. Apparently they had no relatives and led an isolated life. He did not know why they had not had more children, but it was not part of the family ethos to discuss issues that involved emotions. Mr A had grown up feeling isolated and relying mainly on his school peers for company.

He had been in therapy with me for nearly two years when he heard that another boy had reported the choirmaster to the Police, that is, some twenty years after the events. Mr A was called and gave his testimony. Apparently, he was not too disturbed by this. After some weeks, the Police officer who had interviewed him, called him back to clarify some points of his report. Somehow, once this was sorted out, Mr A plucked up the courage and asked whether other boys had been more abused than he had been—and, apparently, the officer nodded, saying this seemed to be the case. Reporting this in his therapy session, Mr A found it very difficult to contain his tears. The officer's response had shaken him: he could not cope with the discovery that, contrary to the deep and intense feelings he had for the choirmaster, he had not really had any special meaning in the choirmaster's life.

This case brought back to me the memory of a young lady in her late teens that I had treated as an in-patient in a Psychiatric Adolescent Unit. She had been admitted because of a serious depression she had developed when her father died, unexpectedly, of a heart attack. At one of our individual therapy sessions, she told me that her father had abused her sexually since her late childhood. I could hardly hide my surprise and, with difficulty, asked her how it was that this had obviously not upset her. She was now crying and, painfully, said, "When Dad died I lost the only person who had ever loved me."

Ms H

Ms H was in her late twenties and held a senior position in a lawyers' firm. She had had two earlier relationships that had broken down after a few years and when she came to see me for a consultation, she had been living on her own for some two or three years. But some weeks before our meeting, a very beloved nephew had been admitted to hospital with liver cancer and this was still giving rise to enormous anxiety. Ms H cried painfully when recounting her nephew's illness. When she finally managed to move on in her account, she mentioned having a one night sexual affair with a man she had just met at a friend's party—something she had never engaged in. As she added that she had not had any sexual encounter since her last relationship had come to an end, I said to her that she probably had not sought sex that evening, but instead had sought life.

Ms H burst out crying again. This was a different, quieter cry. And she said "How true! The most perceptive and helpful thing I have been told in many years!"

This is a precious illustration of the point I made above, where words are used while the person seems to have no awareness of the unconscious feelings that underlie their particular choice of words. Having the good luck to identify those feelings brings insight and relief. If Ms H had felt guilt and shame for her sexual encounter, she could now recognise how traumatised she had been by her nephew's illness.

Mr Morris

This was an accountant in his early forties who was having psychotherapy sessions to help him overcome a number of situations that provoked anxiety crises. Very intelligent and articulate, he was successful in his work and kept in touch with a wide network of friends and colleagues. But his relationships with women repeatedly landed him in situations where he could not make sense of his feelings and impulses. At the time Mr Morris was seeing me he was involved with Marianne, whom he described as very beautiful and lovely. Some time earlier he had discovered that she had had an affair while they were already going out together—but, somehow, he forgave her and they continued their relationship.

But it was the sexual side of this relationship that justifies this presentation. However close they were from an emotional point of view, Mr Morris was unable to get an erection and Marianne protested bitterly about this. However, they discovered that when she took the initiative for having sex and massaged him, they both got excited and he was able to achieve an erection and ensure that both reached climaxes.

Time went on, sex was not a frequent topic of Mr Morris' sessions, but I knew that his relationship with Marianne had become more "serious": he visited her parents, they all spent holidays together. But one day … something changed and Mr Morris now began to voice dissatisfaction, reluctance to prolong the relationship with Marianne. They had unprotected sex, but he now said he did not find her sexually attractive. And one day he finally told me details of their sexual encounters: Marianne enjoyed snogging. Not only enjoyed, but she demanded it and they would snog for up to an hour, until she would achieve an orgasm.

I failed to control myself and said that this was an unusual form of oral sex ... I soon found that Mr Morris had only managed to tell me of Marianne's demands because he had reached the point of not being willing to sustain their relationship and he left her a few weeks after this session. Not long afterwards he decided to travel abroad and this put an end to our meetings.

Solomon

A pharmacist in his late forties, Solomon requested a consultation, wanting my advice over the advisability of psychotherapy. His parents had a stormy relationship, father had died years earlier and his mother "was still alive, always something of a dreaded dictator". Solomon only managed to face marriage after he was forty years old, but this collapsed after two years. A couple of years later, he married again and just over one year before seeing me, his second wife had lost a pregnancy achieved through IVF. This wife was now forty-five years old and she had an adolescent daughter. Mrs S was very keen to have another child and Solomon was happy to support her.

We discussed these features of his history and then Solomon told me that he could not ejaculate during sex, only after masturbation. His wife did not mind this; he penetrates, she has an orgasm and then masturbates him. But because Mrs S's eggs are no longer fertile, they are using his sperm to fertilise a surrogate mother.

Clearly, this is a perfect example of how a couple can have a happy, harmonious relationship, whatever the precise details of their sexual life.

Solomon is one of several men I have seen who were unable to ejaculate during penetrative sex: all of them having been brought up by "dictator", possessive mothers.

Mr Jackson

This computer expert was in his late thirties when he came to see me. He felt caught up in a very long-term relationship, where brief periods of closeness were followed by long months of distance—and yet, much the same way as his partner, Mr Jackson was not able to reach a decision on whether to get married or to move away for good. Listening to his account, it was quite remarkable to hear how similar their lives were. His partner was several years older than he was, though only recently had he discovered that this was the case. Both of them were severely addicted to alcohol. They had shared very painful experiences when the lady suffered from miscarriages, but time and again their love for each other would help them cope with the pain.

Quite often Mr Jackson would refer to his fear of "losing control". Because of his athletic body build, I always assumed he was referring to physical attacks. But one day he made a point of stressing that, however disturbed by his partner's behaviour, he might use foul language, but he would never attack her physically. In fact, he had never been involved in fights of any kind. I was intrigued by this and put it to him that it was difficult to understand his anxiety about losing control being so real, so intense: was it possible that earlier in his life, perhaps in his childhood, he had had some experience where he felt he *had* lost control?

It turned out that he had had such an experience. During his childhood, he was not sure what age, but over two years or so, when his father left for work in the early hours of the morning, he would go to his parents' bed and he would play games with his mother. He remembered vividly how very often she would lie on top of him and he was unable to breathe freely and how he felt a huge sense of relief when she moved off, because he could breathe again. But, he stressed, the point is how intensely he remembered having an erection—and feeling terrified, not being sure whether she knew this had happened.

Quite an unusual experience of "losing control" … and this had certainly laid the ground for the self-image of a person who could "lose control" in other situations. Considering Mr Jackson's unconscious, we could hypothesize that he had chosen a partner who fitted the image he had of his mother. In spite of his words, I still suspected that his alcoholism might lead him to lose control of his physical impulses.

Mr Smith

Though he was nearly thirty years old, Mr Smith had never managed to have actual sex with a woman. He had had many girlfriends and had spent hours together in bed with several of them, but he could not reach an erection. He was now in love with a girl and was keen to discover the reason for his incapacity. He told me of many memories regarding his relationship with his mother. His father was described as "a brute", always tormenting my patient and his older brother, as well as repeatedly involved in violent quarrels with his mother. In fact, his father had hit his wife many times. My patient remembered sitting on the back seat of the family's car, holding the hand that his mother extended to the back.

But the crucial memory came when Mr Smith remembered an evening when the parents had been involved in a terrible fight and then withdrawn to their bedroom. After a little while, his brother called him and tried to take him to the door of the parents' room, to hear the noises they were making. He refused to do so and told me that he had felt relieved, considering that at least the parents could find comfort and togetherness in sex. I reminded him of the saying "it is all in the eyes of the beholder": theoretically, it was also possible to imagine that he had interpreted that their violence had continued in their love-making. To my surprise, Mr Smith had a strong reaction, stuttering and trying to stop tears that were flowing from his eyes. "Oh, God! Perhaps this is why I feel that sex is a violent thing …"

We discussed this finding in further sessions—and Mr Smith was able to lose his virginity with his girlfriend.

The Guardian *newspaper*

On 17 May 2008, in the "Family" section I found this remarkable report:

> Rachel Field, magistrate and former midwife—"The case that really sticks in my mind was a middle-class family in which 3 girls and a boy had all been horrendously sexually abused by their father—a respected member of the community—with the collusion of their alcoholic mother. The abuse only came to light when the eldest told her fiancé … They were fantastic kids; they sat in court holding hands." The eldest married the fiancé and got residence with the youngest two. But the other girl "She was intelligent, sophisticated and wanted to be a lawyer, but she said, 'I love my father and will always support him'". (*The Guardian*, 2008, pp. 4–5)

Here we have one more example of an abused child experiencing the abusing father as a loved or estimated figure. Clearly, ordinary morality rules do not lead to universal followers. As in other similar cases, "knowing" something is incorrect or wrong, does not yet determine that person's emotional experience of the situation in question.

Mr Sutherland

This was a fifty-year-old gentleman, born in the Continent, who lived in London, but because of his work in a financial company travelled a great deal to South America. He was experiencing crises of depression and was referred to me by his GP. His wife was in her late forties, a successful sculptress. They had two children now in their early twenties. Mr Sutherland was certain that both he and his wife had a harmonious and loving relationship. But his account of their sexual life was quite extraordinary.

He told me that his wife was homosexual and she only got involved with married women. In fact, at the time of our meeting, the couple had two lady lodgers in their home—one of which had intimate contact with Mrs Sutherland. Mr Sutherland told me that, whenever he was abroad, he had contact with women—but exclusively with prostitutes.

Mr Sutherland's account of his "happy marriage" confirmed my experience that there is no logic in love. As the saying goes "love is blind", that is, only the couple themselves know what motivates their closeness.

George and Rosemary

These two people in their mid-thirties came to see me together. Indeed, they lived together, but when I used the word "partners", I was corrected: this was not the case. They had been together for some three years, but they wanted me to see them as boyfriend/girlfriend, no more. What kept them together? No, they did not use the word "love", and listening to the accounts of their lives, I could only imagine they experienced some complex kind of mutual resonance that, because of its fragility, had led them to choose the particular "label" they had told me to define their relationship.

George would wake up in the middle of the night and find that he had an erection, but the moment Rosemary spotted this she would burst out in accusations that he was dreaming of other women. But it could happen that if, instead of accusing him, she tried to engage him sexually … the erection disappeared.

George told me that since adolescence, he had discovered that he had erections without being aroused; he recounted waking up with an erection, trying to masturbate and the erection going, so he had to start again, masturbating until he got the erection back. He thought that erections were a mechanism to deal with the distribution of blood. Somehow, the concept of "sex" seemed to be absent. He felt persecuted by his penis; he agreed with my comment that he saw his penis as a foreign body, an enemy.

Rosemary told me that she was the youngest of four children. She had had a boyfriend for five years, but this came to an end when he told her he had met another woman. She told me that "being rejected" was her Achilles' heel, simply devastating to her. She considered George an incurable tormentor, while he felt himself persecuted by both Rosemary and his penis. Much to my surprise, they told me that they would "not dream" of arousing each other, so that repeatedly she challenged him—and it all went wrong.

Nevertheless, I was certainly not prepared to learn the next chapter: it occurred that Rosemary would often lose control and start hitting George, while he was just terrified that he might suddenly lose control and hit her back. And finally the last line: her former boyfriend used to hit her throughout all the five years the relationship had lasted …

George and Rosemary were leaving London soon after our meeting. I was seeing this couple in the eighties, so I told them of the Johnson and Masters technique, very fashionable at that time, where the couple would explore the body parts of each other, but never, ever allow themselves to move on to engage in sex. Research had shown that after a few such exercises, most couples were able to accept their own and each other's sexual feelings and proceed to engage in penetrative sex.

I had found them an interesting and likeable couple; but George was incredibly naïve and I thought Rosemary was sweet, but frail. I was quite convinced that they would remain together—but with very little, or no room for change. Indeed a negative prognosis, but this is based on the fact that over the three years they were together, this couple seemed to have developed a *modus vivendi* that appeared to meet the unconscious needs of both of them. Rosemary and George seemed to have a total incapacity to say "enough!" and move on. Rosemary's previous five-year relationship was another pointer to her difficulty in breaking off traumatic emotional links.

I can only hope that I was wrong in my assessment.

Valerie

I saw this thirty-year-old lady for a health insurance assessment, since she was starting psychotherapy with a colleague. She was very thin and incredibly beautiful, with a captivating, almost disturbing smile. Valerie seemed ready to tell me her history and I found myself wondering about the veracity of such disturbing experiences as she claimed to have gone through.

Valerie was "father's girl" and her older brother of two years was her mother's favourite. Valerie had baths together with her father and he often had an erection. She was "involved with sex" from age four to eleven: she did not go into details about this, but stressed that she had never been penetrated. Father was "very violent" and would often hit Valerie and her brother. She described her mother as "belonging to an old generation", meaning that all these daily events were accepted as normal. However, at around eleven years of age, Valerie told her mother about what she was going through and the sexual encounters seem to have reduced in frequency. She was crying copiously while telling me of these events.

She moved to London, away from her family and soon got involved with a married man, a colleague at work. They became engaged, but he changed his mind, going back to his family. The relationship, however, continued and she made a point of mentioning the large size of his penis.

Valerie went on to meet another young man, "terribly obsessed with sex", with whom she would "have sex" for many uninterrupted hours. Again surprising me, she found it important to specify that most of this sex involved her gratifying his desires, inserting something into his anus.

Valerie had used enormous amount of drugs. With all her sexual activities it was not surprising to learn of an abortion in her mid-teens. She later had a tubal pregnancy and it happened that at the time of our meeting she knew she was pregnant—but not sure who the father was.

I urged Valerie to pursue psychotherapy. Her potential abilities deserved effective help and I hope she did obtain this in due course.

Francis

Born in the Continent, Francis came to England in his mid-twenties to work in a branch of the building company that had employed him from late adolescence. I saw him when he was in his mid-thirties, following a referral from a GP. Francis had seen quite a number of analysts in his life, each one adopting different number of sessions per week and going on for several years before Francis decided to move on to another analyst: either because of moving countries or else to search for new changes.

Francis was a likeable, handsome, and intelligent young man. His life experiences ... well, nobody would ever guess those unless he decided to reveal them. His parents were alive and they had gone through a serious crisis when Francis was ten years old: his father had an affair with the housemaid and his mother went on to have a serious breakdown, remaining on psychiatric medications until the time Francis was seeing me.

A brother who was ten years older than Francis had abused him after the age of nine: "he didn't rape me, because I allowed him". This brother had "never got it right in life" and ended up committing suicide. Another sibling, a sister, seemed to be leading a "normal" married life, bringing up her children.

Francis found his way to Art College and also to a religious Church. Not surprisingly, he achieved positions of prestige, developing his artistic and intellectual potentials. All through these years Francis was involved with several women, but never having actual sex with any of them—and struggling with his homosexual desires. At one point, visiting the USA, he picked up a Congolese man and a few days later happened to slip when walking in a park and fractured an arm: he took it as God's punishment. But he still went on to have further casual homosexual encounters.

At the time of our consultation, Francis was moving towards marriage with a lady friend. He had struggled with feelings of attraction towards one of her brothers (who was gay) and he had told his fiancée about his homosexuality—but she "did not mind it" and they had quite an active sexual life. Considering this development, I asked him if he "felt fulfilled?" Francis thought for a little while and muttered: "no". His facial expression and body posture seemed to indicate puzzlement about his apparent lack of emotional gratification at this approaching step.

Francis was due to travel abroad shortly for his honeymoon and also as part of work. He had great difficulty in affording private fees and eventually he was offered a vacancy to be treated by a trainee in a training psychotherapy organisation.

Doris

This young lady was in her mid-twenties when I met her. She felt "unhappy, depressed" and a friend suggested she should consult me.

She had come to the UK a couple of years earlier and while working as an au pair she met Stephen and fell in love with him. Doris took him to her country of origin and her family had "fallen in love" with him. Some two months before seeing me she had decided to marry Stephen—in spite of the long series of complaints she went on to voice in our meeting.

Doris described her father as "a zero, nothing", while mother was an enterprising and successful nurse. Doris had tried to study literature and later nursing, but had given up on both and tried to "find her way" in England. She had a couple of boyfriends, but Stephen had captivated her. She described him as "strict and unimaginative". As for sex, when she "wanted oral sex" he refused it, saying it was pornographic, in spite of frequently demanding she should do this to him—"I do it … I am very submissive, no?"

Stephen ran a very profitable company. He had an expensive car and other luxuries; he went out to drink and spend time with friends and often mocked and humiliated her in front of them. As she told me about this, she added "but I love him …" He had taken her to meet his parents, but never told them of their intention to get married. Doris was now determined to "start and finish a career" and she hoped I would help her achieve this. Somehow, I could not imagine Doris pursuing therapy regularly. I thought that, for some reason I could not fathom, she was stuck in a self-abasement position and could not find her way out of it.

Doris came to see me again two weeks later. Again a stream of complaints about Stephen endlessly ignoring and humiliating her privately and when with friends—"but I love him …" She told me of what she considered "the difference between having sex and making love": even if having sex every night, she seldom enjoyed it, she could not relax, couldn't ask him for "what I really want". And soon—"but I love Stephen". We had to finish the session and, much to my surprise, she now told me she was travelling to her home country, where she would spend two months so that she could have plastic surgery, reducing the size of her breasts: "they just hang down … I want to have them firmer." I presume she wanted to give me a clearer image of the culture in which she had spent her earlier life, as she added: "back home, men only want meat—breasts and buttocks!"

I must confess that I was not surprised when Doris did not contact me again. Needing help? Surely. But wanting help? I somehow suspected she did not "want" it or could not believe she might achieve changes in her life that might improve her self-image. Seeing Doris was quite a painful experience and I could not forget how, at one point, she had told me that many times in her life people had told her she was "stupid". What prevented her from seeking change? I did not manage to help Doris.

Saul

This gentleman and his wife were having marital therapy with a colleague of mine and she suggested he should consult me. Saul was in his early fifties and held a very senior position in a building society. Mary, his wife, was a few years younger than him and ran an information technology firm. They had been living together for over fifteen years, but had never got married because Mary was against such a procedure. They had two sons, both leading normal, successful lives.

Saul told me of his personal history and of two earlier long-term relationships with other women. Both these two love affairs had finished when the women decided they were not satisfied with their relationship with Saul. He described Mary as a highly unstable lady, frequently losing her temper and at times making derogatory comments about Saul to friends and relatives. She had been severely traumatised at the birth of their younger son and, whether as a consequence or a coincidence, the couple stopped their sexual life.

It happened that Saul's sexual life had always followed an unusual pattern. With both long-term lovers and with occasional partners sex involved various manoeuvres, but not actual penetration. Women accepted this—except for the two lovers who reached a point of dissatisfaction and broke off the relationship. Saul's description of his present life with Mary clearly implied that she had accepted his approach to sexuality. And this is the point that explains my recounting this story. They slept together, they might kiss and hug each other, Mary did not seem to care whether they had sex or not, but sometimes Saul decided that he wanted intercourse: but he discovered that he could not produce an erection. His earlier non-penetrative sex was a choice, a decision, but now this was not the case: and he could not understand this development.

I decided to call Saul's attention to the fact that previous women had left him—he seemed quite incapable of finishing, stopping a relationship and, then, taking into account his description of Mary's general behaviour toward him, I suggested that the lack of an erection could well be his penis doing what he was incapable of doing. Saul froze and he had tears coming to his eyes.

I saw Saul for a few more sessions and his incapacity to stop a relationship was the main theme of our discussions. He gradually felt less anxious, but there was no significant change in his relationship with Mary.

Benedict

This gentleman applied for a psychotherapy vacancy in a training organisation and I saw him to assess his suitability for this. He was in his early forties and earned his living by doing commissioned writing for a publishing firm. He had no particular physical feature that would strike someone meeting him. He clearly had an impressive command of language, but his emotional posture and tone of voice were remarkably smooth and flat.

Benedict was one of four children and his mother had suffered a miscarriage after the second child was born—but I was not able to ascertain if this had any significance in his development. He had been involved in two long-term relationships and was now living with a girlfriend. They had known each other for eight years and had been living together for five years.

Benedict told me about his much-loved two-year-old daughter, "marvellous, very gifted, precious". He also mentioned that pregnancy had been an accident, but there was no indication in his tone of voice that this had any special meaning. I ended up deciding to ask him what sex meant to him. It was his answer that I found so striking: Benedict told me of "two kinds of sex—one is where both parties just want to enjoy it, and another where love is the main factor". But I could not avoid the impression that here was one more example of Benedict's rich command of language. He mentioned how much he "wants to give" and values "being wanted", but I did not have the courage to check on my impression that, at least since the birth of their daughter, both types of sex were conceptual formulations, with no actual sexual life existing in the couple's life.

I felt that Benedict was a suitable person to be seen by a psychotherapy trainee. I was not totally convinced about his capacity for insight, but he was very motivated and I recommended he should be offered a vacancy.

Francisca

I was visiting Portugal when a colleague asked me to see this forty-five-year-old lady. There was no question of "therapy"; it was rather that she was struggling with feelings that she did not feel able to discuss with anyone in her community—in Portuguese you might say she needed to have a "desabafo", some loading off, a release from the tension, anxiety, pain, that she had resigned herself to the impossibility of eliminating.

Hearing her account produced complex and disturbing emotions in me. She cried throughout our ninety-minute meeting, struggling to keep her feelings and thoughts under control. She had never met an analyst or therapist: not part of the community in which she lived. Her father had died four years earlier, suddenly, unexpectedly, and though no autopsy had been carried out, it was accepted that he had suffered acute heart failure.

Francisca was in her early twenties when she became engaged to a man she loved. Sadly, the car he was driving crashed and he had a cervical vertebra fracture that left him paralysed from the neck down. A miracle happened: he managed to obtain a literature degree and was able to write reviews and original texts, with the continuous assistance of Francisca. He could not sustain erections but they managed, somehow, to have some form of sex for a few years, but he lost interest in this. It was three years before our meeting that this unhappy man "managed to die" after a lung infection that developed into a complicated clinical picture: tracheotomy, brain damage, and coma. Francisca and his family begged doctors to allow him to die, but they refused to do it.

The question arises: why did Francisca never leave him? "I loved him, he was a wonderful man". I thought I had to ask about the question of children. And much to my surprise, Francisca told me that they had made many attempts at IVF with her partner's sperm, but unfortunately she had never actually become pregnant.

At the time of our meeting Francisca had met, and would often go out with, a married man who kept telling her that he would leave his wife if and when Francisca wanted to marry him. But he had an unstable mood and often got very drunk and abusive. I could not hide my surprise. A married man? A man who got drunk and abusive? I thought she was clearly exposing herself to further pain and frustration. I was very careful in choosing my words, but I made profuse apologies and told Francisca she should move away from this man. I also urged her to find an analyst who could help her to cope more effectively with all her pain and achieve a smoother menopause.

CHAPTER TWO

Unusual solutions

These are stories from my work in the NHS as a Child and Adolescent Psychiatrist. They are being described because of the manner in which the presenting symptom came to be eliminated—not the usual textbook recommended therapy, but some unexpected comment or recommendation that enabled the patient to overcome his complaint—and sometimes not my intervention. Sadly, these were solutions that could not simply be implemented with the next difficult patient, but I found them fascinating lessons of some children's empathy and creativity. I believe they are well worth recounting.

Michael

Michael developed school phobia. He was eleven years old and had always been successful in his school and social life. But when the new school term started, he claimed to be feeling ill and refused to leave the house. His parents were not particularly worried, but days went by and Michael still refused to go to school, putting forward all kinds of excuses. As some of these involved body experiences (abdominal colic, chest pains, dizziness, nightmares, etc.) the parents took him to the GP.

A physical examination revealed no pathology and tests were negative. The GP was, however, concerned because both Michael's parents had been going through a series of severe illnesses and he thought this might be provoking Michael's anxiety-related complaints.

Eventually, the GP decided to refer Michael to the local Child Guidance Clinic. When I saw Michael and his parents, I found him an articulate, intelligent boy who knew to answer all my questions and sustain a friendly dialogue with his parents. They were very concerned over their son's complaints, not convinced at all by the negative results of tests or by the GP's words of reassurance. Amid the multitude of illnesses these parents were struggling with, I was particularly struck by the fact that Mr M had recently had a heart attack from which he was still recovering. He had gone back to work, but this aroused considerable anxiety in his wife because he insisted on getting there driving his motorcycle.

Considering the information obtained from the GP that no physical pathology had been found to justify Michael's complaints and the apparent link between Mr M's heart attack and the beginning of Michael's school phobia, I decided to suggest that it might be worth Mr M driving Michael to school on his motorbike when going to work. They thought this was a funny suggestion, but with considerable laughter decided they would "give it a try".

So they did, and when we had a follow-up meeting two weeks later, I learnt that Michael had now resumed his school attendance, with no further problems.

Presumably, it was Michael's anxiety regarding his father's dangerous life situation that led to his fear of finding himself away from home if or when something happened to his father—but being driven to school by Mr M produced the required reassurance that his father was now safely "in control" of his life.

Henry

Henry was eight years old and he led a very successful social and school life, but he had not managed to overcome his enuresis. He would wet himself in his sleep and also during the daytime, producing considerable anxiety. Not managing to help Henry, the GP referred him to a Paediatrician, who eventually sent him to a Urologist—they had not managed to find any physical pathology, and the prescribed medication as well as various kinds of advice had produced no results. Eventually, I was asked to see Henry.

I found him a likeable, friendly boy, well able to put his anxieties into words, but I was unable to identify any underlying unconscious fantasy that might be preventing Henry from controlling the function of his sphincter. Mrs H, who had brought her son to see me, did not hide her frustration and anger at the persistence of Henry's enuresis. She answered my questions and occasionally commented on something Henry had said. But when we were about to finish our meeting, she just exploded "he goes on behaving like a little boy who needs to sleep in nappies!" Henry was deeply embarrassed, but I did not manage to stop myself from laughing at this formulation. I said that perhaps Mrs H was right and that she should follow her intuition, putting a nappy on Henry when he was going to bed. Henry jumped! "You wouldn't do it, would you?" and Mrs H retorted "Of course I would: no, I will!" Henry was crestfallen. I told Mrs H that she should introduce a chart, counting the nights when Henry wet himself or, instead, managed to control his sphincter—and to give him a reward after an agreed number of dry nights.

I was left wondering what would happen … When they came to see me two weeks later Mrs H was proud and delighted and Henry showed me the prize his mother had given him: he had not wet himself a single time after our meeting. I must confess that I could not have predicted the result of my recommendation. Considering its success, I believe that by putting the nappies on Henry, Mrs H was demonstrating that her previous considerate and supposedly loving manner of treating him resulted from her belief that he was incapable of changing and acquiring control of his sphincter. However, the moment she forced him to wear the nappies led him to feel, quite unconsciously, that his mother now believed that he had the potential of "growing up" and behaving in an age-appropriate manner.

We have here an example of the vicious circle where the parent's assessment of the child's symptoms leads to the child unconsciously interpreting the parent's input as proof that there is some abnormality in his body—and the persistence of the symptom leads the parent to see it as confirmation of his/her reading of the child's problem. I do believe that it was the change in Mrs H's manner of treating Henry that enabled him to overcome his unconscious conviction that there was "something wrong" in his body.

George

George was just under three years old when referred to me because of his "impossible" bad behaviour and frequent vomiting episodes. The GP had not found any physical problems that might be causing the vomiting and suggested the family should consult me at the Child Guidance. I found George a smiling, friendly boy who chose to play at the dolls house with great interest. He came to our meeting with his father and paternal grandmother, who told me of George's life experiences: his mother had left Mr G, taking George to live with her and a lover. Soon Mr G discovered that this lover was beating up his wife and threatening to hurt George. He managed to obtain custody of the boy, but now neither Mr G nor his mother could make sense of George's behaviour.

In his daily life, George was able to entertain himself with various toys and he engaged in conversation with the adults, but occasionally he spoke of "a man hitting people" and showed signs of anxiety. But Mrs G could not make sense, for example, of George refusing to eat food served to him, demanding it was prepared in a special way. Furthermore, he quite often became clearly worried and tense, soon vomiting whatever he had eaten. She described George as "demanding, manipulative".

From my experience with children in similar situations, I suggested that he was not "manipulating" them, but rather testing them out, hoping they would not punish him by getting rid of him—as he most probably felt he had lost his mother. Their reaction surprised me. Both Mr G and his mother went on to describe how, as soon as one of them indicated they were going out, George would bombard them with anxious questions, wanting to be reassured that they would come back.

I suggested to Mr G and his mother that they really needed to ignore George's experiences with his mother and, instead, treat him like "a normal child". Their attempts to pamper, pacify, and protect George were "backfiring" and increasing his fears. I suggested that the vomiting was the climax of these feelings of insecurity and that they should try to spot George's anxiety at an early point and deal with him as they would with any "normal" child: they should stop and urge him to explain what was bothering him—this type of comforting might avoid the boy's anxiety mounting to the point of "needing" to vomit.

Mr G and his mother did manage to change their approach to George—and there were no further episodes of vomiting.

Thomas

Thomas was seven years old when I saw him. He had enormous difficulties going to sleep and the family had tried to help in many ways—so had the GP, but trouble prevailed. This case did have an unusual and successful solution, but not my achievement! Both parents brought Thomas and his brother James, aged nine, for the consultation. I took the family history and then Thomas told me of what tormented him: he was obsessed with a ghost who threatened to kill him from the moment he began to fall asleep. Both parents and James described the night-time events and while they sympathised with Thomas, they found it hard to suppress a smile at the specific content of his fears. I asked Thomas to make drawings and tried to discuss how he had come to imagine the figure of the ghost—but I did not find my way to any meaningful interpretation of his anxieties. We ended up making another appointment for two weeks later.

When we next met, the family were delighted to see me and very keen to break their news: Thomas was now sleeping normally, no further ghosts threatening him. How did this happen? What was the solution? "Oh!" the proud parents said, "It was James who did it!" And I turned to James. "Well … one night, Thomas began to cry and shout, I went to the window, opened it wide and screamed 'Stupid ghost: get out of here!' and turned to Thomas and said 'did you see? He flew away!' And that was it … no more problems …"

I thought that the vital difference in the various approaches we had all had to Thomas was the fact that only his brother conveyed to him that he *believed* in the "reality" of the ghost. And this brought me to the realisation that our usual well-intentioned attempts at reassurance and comforting very often carry the implication that we do not really believe in the "reality" of our patient's or child's fear. In other words, our ordinary efforts to help the patient (or anyone) often put him in the position of *feeling inclined or bound* to trust our words, but still not knowing what these views have to do with his underlying overwhelming anxiety. If an example is required, I would mention our fruitless efforts in trying to convince children (and adults!) that they do not truly *need* to wash their hands so often or check so many times whether they have, in fact, properly locked a door. Their facial expression will usually show their suspicion that we are not interested in what worries them, but only wish to eliminate behaviour that upsets or irritates us.

Tony

Tony's story is described in the chapter on "Unusual stories", but our interviews brought to light a fascinating exchange between Tony and his sister. When I met Tony and his mother for a follow-up interview, our conversation focused on the question of nightmares. She told me that both she and Mr T had suffered from nightmares in their early years, adding "perhaps this is why (we) responded so keenly to Tony's night-time behaviour". But she then went on to tell me of a wonderful episode: one night Tony's sister woke up in a panic, terrified by a monster that was under her bed—and Tony told her "simple! You just switch on the light and the monster dies!" And the girl went to sleep quite peacefully … I see this comment being so effective because the girl's fear is not dismissed or ignored: instead Tony's words imply a belief in the truth of her experience.

Lucy

Lucy found it difficult to fall asleep and often complained of nightmares, but the main reason for the parents to consult me was the frequency with which she was found to be masturbating. They told me that this abnormal behaviour appeared to be linked to the birth, eight months earlier, of her youngest brother. Prior to this, Lucy was seen as a normally developing, very intelligent, and sociable little girl, though she had also started to "steal" things, both at home and school. Lucy had told her parents that she "wished she was a baby" and they took this as confirmation of their impression that Lucy felt envious of her brother's "privileges". I was impressed by the manner in which Mrs L had dealt with Lucy's stealing: she had told Lucy that "perhaps instead of stealing things that can get you into trouble, it might be best if you talked to me"—and the stealing had ceased.

Lucy aged eight, and her four-and-a-half-year-old brother had friends, two brothers of the same ages and they often had baths together. And one day Lucy came to her mother, clearly full of delight and enthusiasm "I've also got a willy!" Mrs L carefully asked Lucy to show her this "willy" and very gently told her that this was a clitoris, since girls do not have willies. Lucy was clearly disappointed—but, to the parents' puzzlement, her "masturbation" did not stop. When they told me this story, I could not stop myself from laughing. The parents were surprised by this and I said "I think Lucy is trying to stretch her clitoris!"

Mr and Mrs L clearly did not know what to make of my words and politely asked me how they should proceed. Did I want them to bring Lucy to see me? I said that, considering how Mrs L had managed to dissuade Lucy from stealing, I would suggest that, provided she agreed with my interpretation, she should discuss this with her daughter. Only if this did not achieve a change would I ask to see Lucy. Considering that these parents worked in health related fields, I added that perhaps they should also ask their GP whether it was possible that Lucy was suffering from Oxyuris infection.

Lucy's parents contacted me two weeks later: Mrs L had discussed with Lucy her possible desire to stretch her clitoris—and the masturbation had ceased …

Peter

Peter was a twelve-year-old boy who was presenting odd behaviour both at home and in the community. It was the school that decided the boy required a psychological assessment. The Educational Psychologist diagnosed psychotic behaviour and the boy was referred to the Child Guidance Clinic. When I saw him, Peter addressed me as any other normal young adolescent might do. Eventually, I said I could not really understand why the school and psychologist had been worried about him. He looked a bit embarrassed and told me that at times he would "see" distortions in people and things around him, and also find ideas that he knew were absurd "taking over" his thoughts, making him afraid that he might be going crazy and, understandably, this fear produced further intense anxious feelings. He was seeing me with his mother. They came from a Far Eastern country and were devoted practitioners of their religion. They led a perfectly normal life and were well settled into the local community. I was finding it quite difficult to make sense of Peter's "hallucinations", since his description of these appeared to be so discordant with the general picture of his personality. As the interview was coming to an end, Peter's mother asked to see me on her own.

Mrs P wanted to tell me that her son's problems had started some months after, in line with the family's religious practices, he had been circumcised two years earlier. Following the surgical procedure, in line with the surgeon's recommendations, twice a day she would wash and clean her son's prepuce. But she had continued to perform this cleaning, even if she could see that the skin had healed perfectly. And she asked me whether she was justified in continuing to do it. As gently as possible, I told her she should stop doing it.

Follow-up information was that the psychotic behaviour disappeared and when I offered another appointment, I was given their thanks but told that no further meetings were necessary.

From an academic point of view we can indeed wonder about the specific form with which Peter's unconscious "chose" to express its anxieties and impulses. Do we consider the hallucinations as self-limited, strictly linked to his particular emotional circumstances? Or should we take them as indications of an instinctual vulnerability that might surface again? Certainly from a pragmatic point of view there was nothing else that could/should be implemented. Only later consultations might allow us to confirm the correctness of this viewpoint, but I had no further information about Peter's development.

Herbert

I was asked to see this nine-year-old boy because he was complaining of nightmares and of a constant fear that he or someone in the family might die. This meant running to his mother's bed every night and staying there, in spite of her attempts to reassure him.

I saw Herbert together with his mother. Father's work timetable had prevented him from joining us. Mrs H voiced her sense of helplessness, but it was very clear that she shared most of her son's anxieties. Herbert expressed his fear in a simple way: "I'm afraid that one day I'll wake up and find that I'm dead!" His mother's anxieties came across in an equally explicit and detailed way. Both she and Mr H came from religious families and some of their relatives had joined religious sects that departed dramatically from the "proper" religion of their original family. But there was another element to the family's devotion and present pleads to God: a very large number of relatives had died of cancer and some were facing chronic incapacitating illnesses.

Herbert told me of his daily life. School was good, seeing that teachers and colleagues liked him. He had good friends, but it was his older siblings that tormented him with their mockery of his fears. I tried to check how far did Herbert see the difference between knowing and believing. It was reassuring to find that he could grasp that difference, but he made it clear that he saw all his family as "believers" who were constantly fighting threats.

I decided to try one of my favourite formulations. I asked Herbert: "you go to your GP, he examines you and tells you there is nothing wrong and tells you to come back a few months later if the problem continues—now, another view: your GP examines you and tells you there is nothing wrong, but, who knows? Just in case … let's do a few tests. Is there a difference?"

And much to my delight, Herbert beamed and jumped: "oh, God! The first is easy, small—but the second is really big!" But it turned out that Mrs H did not understand my story and, in fact, seemed to feel angry, thinking I was belittling their anxieties. I tried hard to explain to Mrs H that the more she tried to comfort Herbert, the more he became convinced that there was a *real* possibility of tragedy hitting him. I urged her to not allow Herbert to sleep on her bed—talk to him, but take him back to his own bed. I suggested they should agree on a reward that Herbert would get after sleeping a particular number of nights on his own bed.

Though we arranged a follow-up meeting, Mrs H phoned to cancel it and thanked me for "solving the problem". Herbert was a happier boy and managed to sleep through the nights—and she felt relieved, finally convinced that her son was perfectly normal and healthy.

CHAPTER THREE

Unusual stories

This is a collection of cases where unusual episodes were described. Indeed they "belonged" to that individual's whole life, but these experiences had a striking element when considered in the particular context of that person's life when I met them. Not surprisingly, it was some "symptom" complaint that led to them being referred to see me. This symptom could only be overcome when its significance within the context of that point in the person's life was identified—and significant changes implemented. Some cases responded to our consultation alone, but others required long-term therapy.

David

This family were visiting relatives in London and, at their recommendation, decided to consult me about problems with their eight-year-old-son, David. I had a long conversation with Mrs D over the phone and this was followed by an interview with David and both parents. They seemed to feel that our meeting had been helpful, but they soon went back to their home in the West of England and I had no follow-up to our session. This consultation is being described because of some fascinating, if painful, features that emerged when we met.

Mrs D was in her mid-forties, a senior journalist, particularly interested in the arts. For many years she had resident maids, who looked after the house and the children while she went to other cities or concentrated on her office work. The present maid had approached Mrs D complaining that David had warned her that his mother intended to fire her and that he was reporting her to the Police—he knew that this maid was an immigrant that the Ds were helping to gain legal status to stay in the UK.

Mrs D came to see me together with her husband and David. I went through various points mentioned in our telephone conversation and I then asked her to give me a picture of her personal history. She burst out crying. She was one of twins: her brother was born first and was very small and she was over nine pounds in weight at birth. Mrs D added "all my life my mother blamed me for bursting all her insides". Her mother was very petite and ought to have had a Caesarean, but this was not done.

Mrs D was already a successful journalist when she got married at thirty-four. "I felt I was running away from becoming a mother—my mother was definitely not a model to be followed". And even after she had two children she felt she was "avoiding them". Now that David was so unhappy and presenting problems, she was, not surprisingly, blaming herself for this.

Mr D was an only child, always happy and easy-going. He enjoyed his work as a doctor, had had several relationships, but the day he met Mrs D he was convinced she would be his wife. He described his younger son as calm and placid ("he takes after me"), while David "is temperamental ... labile as is my wife". Both Mr and Mrs D emphasised how they felt that theirs was a happy marriage.

David found it difficult to deal with the meeting and my eventual questions. He was happy with his school and social life. He was very fond of his brother and all their friends. After a while, one of his parents mentioned David's blanket. He was always very attached to it and the parents had replaced it twice, though David kept them "in a safe place". But one day David threw his blanket out of the window. Mr D and the maid wanted to go out and get it, but they were stopped by David's outburst: "I wanted to TEACH IT a lesson!" He was completely unable to explain what he meant, but Mrs D put it to him that perhaps it was *someone* that he had wanted to throw out. Amazingly, David thought for a minute and said this was probably correct, because a couple of days earlier she had been unfair and punitive to him. Clearly, in spite of her poor self-image, Mrs D was a very empathic and insightful person. She went on to say that it was quite possible that David's threats to the maid were the result of his hope that if they had no maid, perhaps he would have a closer relationship with his mother.

I felt that David would benefit from individual psychotherapy. Considering his age, one would expect him to realise that it was not appropriate to threaten the maid in such a hurtful way, much as we would not imagine that an eight-year-old child would "teach a lesson" to his security blanket, particularly when he was apparently aware of how strongly he had resented his mother's way of treating him. Only further observation would allow us to know if he had the capacity to assess which of his feelings were based on reality and, therefore, safe to be expressed.

I urged the parents to find a trustworthy professional in the area where they lived, so that David's progress could be followed. Unfortunately, I did not hear from the family again.

Margaretta

This was an Italian social worker aged thirty-nine who used to consult me in a supervisory capacity to discuss some clients on her caseload. One day she was particularly tense and eventually managed to tell me that she was disappointed, tired, frustrated, and fed up with her analyst. She had been seeing him for two years, but it did not matter what she said, he would promptly throw at her a transference interpretation. She was getting desperate about her wish to have a child, but she kept choosing men who did not want to become more closely involved with her: and the analyst would respond to this sentiment with an interpretation that she resented his keeping distant from her.

A few minutes after telling me this story she moved on the chair on which she was sitting and made a defensive movement. She explained that she suffered from back pains, usually triggered off by wrong movements. I expressed my sympathy and she told me that when she was seventeen years old she suffered an accident and had broken a leg. This required endless surgical interventions that left her with a frail lower spinal column.

Even though numerous years had gone by, her tone of voice indicated how raw and vivid this trauma was in her mind. I somehow plucked up the courage to apologise about my being a doctor and wanting to ask her a question: as she went through these surgeries, did she ever believe she would one day be able to carry the weight of a pregnancy? She shook her head—"No … I thought about it and I was convinced that I would never be a mother". I said that this might be a factor that influenced her choice of men she got involved with. She looked very surprised.

When I next saw Margaretta, she could not stop telling me how grateful she was: in that one meeting I had helped her more than the years she had had of analysis. She also told me how surgeons had said to her that the accident had so profoundly affected her emotions that she would probably be afraid of having a family. After further quotes from surgeons warning her about the need to watch her movements, I said that they were probably trying to reassure her, but she had obviously taken their words as a life sentence.

Margaretta continued to visit me, but made no further reference to this discussion. Then, one day, less than one year later, she cancelled an appointment and explained that she had been going out with a male friend and they had decided to travel to Spain to introduce her to his parents. Another four months went by and she invited me to their wedding. Not long afterwards, they moved to Spain and soon she got pregnant. When visiting London, Margaretta contacts me to report on her life and work—and proudly describes the development of her son.

Many years have gone by and Margaretta has been happily and proudly raising her son. Needless to say, I never had the courage to ask her how relevant did she think my comment had been to these gratifying developments …

Sonia

This is a very brief account that is presented because I believe it contains complex and conflicting emotions that can be found far too often in our present world. Sonia was a lady in her early fifties who came to see me for psychotherapy sessions that might help her with marital problems. She had three adult children who led successful family and professional lives. At this point in her life she was also looking after her mother, who was now in her eighties and presenting a multitude of physical and emotional problems. Sonia had an older sister who had been born with serious physical and mental abnormalities. One day, Sonia and her mother were talking about their life in London during the Second

World War—they had to go quite often into air-raid shelters, and her mother came to tell Sonia that if she could only rescue one child, she would have rescued Sonia's older sister.

How is one supposed to live with this information? And how to approach that mother when one is in the position of her carer? Quite a whirlpool of emotions! This is the type of configuration that has led me many times to argue that looking after the carer must be part of any helping programme instituted to assist the incapacitated patient. In practice, we do find cases where the patient refuses help, arguing this is unnecessary since their "loving carer" can meet his needs, while the carer may be finding it extremely difficult to cope with her feelings towards the patient.

James

I am sure that James' account of his childhood depicts a problem that many clinicians have met in their practice. When we see the patient as a child, it is impossible to predict how his symptom will affect that individual child's development. And meeting the patient in adolescence or adulthood, it can be quite challenging to investigate and establish whether there is any correlation between the presenting clinical picture and the early childhood problems.

James sought psychotherapy because he felt that a man of his age, thirty-seven, should be more self-confident, better able to face the world in a spontaneous, candid manner. He held an important job in a building company, but his social life was virtually non-existent. He was close to his brother, but held a strong bitterness and hostility to their mother. He felt guilty for such negative feelings, particularly when he felt incapable of explaining their origin.

During his fifth session he suddenly jumped, saying that he had just recovered a memory: as a child, one day he walked through his mother's rose bed. She was furious, calling him "clumsy", which was her customary word for him and punished him for ruining the roses. I asked James if he had bled. He said that yes, his skin was torn and it bled quite badly, but he had no memory of how his mother had dealt with that.

This was the opening of a Pandora's box. James went on to remember and recount endless incidents of crashing on furniture, stumbling on steps, falling down for no known reason, failing to greet someone near him, etc. It was only when James was three and a half years of age that it was finally diagnosed that his vision was severely impaired. Of course, from the moment he started to wear glasses, he began to discover the world around him. Perhaps the fact that the family lived on a farm, quite far away from any neighbouring villages was also an aggravating factor. The result was James growing up with no friends and only mixing with other children when he started at infant school—but even then James could only recall his going to and coming back from school, walking along with his brother.

Knowing of his early childhood visual disturbance, most professionals would consider James' shyness and social isolation as totally understandable, if not predictable. But seen as a child, could we really predict how his adult life would develop? And considering his early years in an isolated community, how relevant would this be to his later shyness?

Christopher

This forty-year-old lawyer consulted me because he wanted to understand, to make sense of, several steps he had taken in the course of his life. He was a successful professional, had a happy marriage and two children growing up with no significant problems. We went through several sessions when Christopher was explaining to me the challenges he had met because of his parents' cultural and religious beliefs. Father and mother came from two different Asiatic countries and were extremely, passionately, devoted to their religion—and this had led them to take it for granted that Christopher would follow a very specific social orientation. When the family moved to the UK, complex and subtle conflicts came to the scene and listening to Christopher it was difficult to understand how his parents had succeeded to maintain a united, loving family.

And so, our sessions went on. We met twice per week and Christopher seemed happy with what he got from my comments and I was often fascinated to learn of a family ethos I had only read about. The point was reached when Christopher said he was happy with what he had learnt and he thought we could stop our sessions. We agreed on a date, but to my total amazement the last two sessions were taken up by Christopher talking about his body, a subject he had not mentioned before.

He had suffered from acne in adolescence and spent hours "squeezing black spots and stuff", ashamed, conscious of his appearance. Then he went on to focus on his eyes: he had had to use glasses from a very young age and had always wished that he could get rid of them. He could not use contact lenses because they were too dry, and he had, therefore, to use ordinary glasses.

But when did this problem start? He was about three when taken to an optician—had enormous trouble, changing many different glasses, until he found one that really helped him to see properly. He explained: "I remember being very clumsy … I used to bump into things and occasionally break something." After a pause, when he looked very thoughtful, he added: "The funny thing is that I used to feel it was my fault … being clumsy, not being able to avoid or correct it". I felt I had to tell him that this was a typical reaction I had met, seeing children with similar problems: they blamed themselves for the consequences of a physical problem that was not being investigated and treated.

So we have two cases where early visual difficulties were handled by their parents in very different ways. And, apparently, quite diverse developments when they moved to adolescence and adulthood. I see the presenting characteristics of their adult lives and the similar childhood disabilities as very powerful warnings that each patient must be evaluated as "an isolated, unique" clinical challenge.

Sylvia

This twenty-three-year-old young lady consulted her GP because of feeling depressed, not managing to cope with the demands of her job and struggling to sustain some degree of a social life. This happened to be an exceptional GP, who, in spite of having known Sylvia for many years, was still prepared to give her the time to express and enlarge on her feelings.

Two years earlier, Sylvia's sister, who was two years older than her, had been found dead. Her sister had threatened to commit suicide many times and had, in fact, taken two overdoses. But one day Sylvia's sister had phoned their mother, who had apologised and said she was busy and agreed for the sister to phone again later. But when no call came and the parents went to the flat where Sylvia's sister lived, they found her dead in the bathtub. Apparently, she had had an epileptic seizure, hit her head on the tub and died.

The GP asked Sylvia whether she had ever felt suicidal herself. Sylvia smiled bitterly and said that her mother kept warning her how devastated she and her father would be if Sylvia ever killed herself. But before the smile faded away, Sylvia said, almost impishly, that when she was fifteen years old she had swallowed an enormous number of tablets that she had found in the house. And much to the GP's surprise, Sylvia added that she eventually found out that, precisely at that same time, her sister was also taking one of her overdoses.

It was very clear to the GP that Sylvia's depression was intimately linked to her feelings about her sister. She was by then crying and finding it difficult to articulate her thoughts. She said how close the two of them were and how competitive she, Sylvia, had been all her life, always trying to match her sister's achievements. Before coming to see the GP, Sylvia had applied to three different universities, and she now knew that each of them had offered her a place. Triumph? Yes, but she added: "What is the point? I cannot really go to the cemetery and tell my sister about this ..."

Predictably, the GP was speechless. What could he say? Competitiveness leads to one kind of comment—loss and pain lead to a totally different type of comment. Psychoanalysts might smile and suggest that these are the two sides of the same coin, two different sentiments bridged together by a sense of guilt. We have, indeed, a large literature on the "feelings of the survivor", but facing someone like Sylvia, all one feels inclined to do is to put a hand on her shoulder and convey one's sympathy.

Sylvia's final remark reminded me of a colleague of mine telling me of a lady friend of his. She was now in her eighties and had just received a precious award for a story she had written. Her reaction? "What is the point of something so good? My husband is no longer here for me to share it with him ..."

George

Quite unusually, George came to one of his psychotherapy sessions feeling very disturbed by a dream he had had the previous night. He could not recall the details, but he woke up shocked when in the dream his left hand was being chopped off.

Now in his early-forties, George was a gifted, creative artist. Inventing techniques, he created his own company, but he also worked with partners in another company. Much to his regret, serious difficulties had arisen in this shared company and he was inclined to leave it, but at the same time he was not certain of the viability of relying on his private company to fulfil all his needs.

We discussed various aspects of his account and of the dream and, eventually, George seemed moved to formulate a summary, but now in good Jewish style. He said: "So, I'm torn … on the one hand (and he raised his right hand) I want to pick up and build up what I created, but (he now raised his left hand) I value what I learnt from my partners …" I stepped in and said that in spite of his words, to judge from the dream it was his present business he was inclined to have "chopped off".

George was shocked. He said I was correct, but he was amazed at the way his unconscious had found to express his feelings.

Marilyn

I have decided to present this brief account because it brought forward one of those frustrating situations where the professional can understand his patient's anxiety, but beyond showing sympathy, he feels as powerless as his patient.

Marilyn was a competent and successful professional in her mid-thirties. She had had a couple of long-term relationships, but as she saw the dreaded fortieth birthday approaching she felt that she had to decide whether to accept or decline her boyfriend's wish that they should have a child. So, what held her back? She had a younger sister who from birth had a series of inherited abnormalities—but their mother had been adopted and, as was the practice in those days, no records were kept of her biological parents.

Not surprisingly, Marilyn did not feel able to risk giving birth to an abnormal child. And what help could I possibly offer? Unfortunately, I do not know what decision Marilyn made, since she cancelled her next appointment.

Daniel

This client was a boy aged eleven, who complained of hearing shouts, echoes, and voices in his head. Both parents were in their early forties; they had got married in the East where they were born and came to England when Mr D was assigned to an executive position in his company. Mrs D had also obtained a senior job as a psychologist. Both of them had several siblings and Daniel was one of the two sons they had.

I never saw Mr D. His wife described him as "a true member of his family: arrogant, bellicose, dictatorial, intolerant". Perhaps not surprisingly, she shrugged her shoulders when telling me that her father was the same type of man.

Daniel looked small for his age and felt quite uncomfortable meeting me, this strange doctor. He eventually told me that he had just learnt that he had gained entry to the same secondary school his older brother attended. I could see that he was an intelligent boy, but he was clearly struggling to answer my questions and tell me of the complaints that had so worried his mother. He had trouble falling asleep, he kept waking up in the night, he was scared of the multiple noises that plagued him, etc., etc. At one point, Daniel mentioned that when these noises hit him at school, he managed to "ignore them", but not when he was at home at night. This remark led me to consider the possibility that Daniel's night-time behaviour indicated his need to check that his mother was available, which led him to "find ways" of staying close to her.

When I mentioned this, I was told that up to one year earlier, Daniel had shared bunk beds with his brother. Not surprisingly, Daniel was delighted when I said to his mother that his problems might improve if the boys shared their bedroom again. I was now sure that Mrs D's attempts to help her son had, in fact, kept his anxieties going.

I next saw Mrs D alone and I learnt why she had come to interpret her son's complaints the way she had done. The brother of a close friend of hers had developed aural hallucinations and psychosis in his mid-teens and it also happened that an older brother of hers had suffered from depression and had committed suicide in his early twenties.

Taking all these findings into consideration, I told Mrs D that Daniel might well benefit from psychotherapy, but perhaps I could see her again to discuss their interaction and observe how our meetings affected Daniel's progress. I went on to see Mrs D for a couple of months. She gradually managed to accept the possibility that her anxieties and her brand of protection and care of Daniel were leading the boy to display behaviour that justified her fears. This insight helped her not to allow Daniel to sleep in her bed and the boy soon stopped getting out of his bed during the night.

Our discussions also allowed Mrs D to understand how, unconsciously, her attachment to Daniel allowed her to feel protected from her husband's intolerable behaviour. She now began to consider whether she would be able to seek a divorce, even if this went against all the principles she had grown up with.

Daniel's hallucinations disappeared and he was very happy in his new school.

Wilson

I have no follow-up to my interviews with Wilson, but I believe he was an immensely gifted young man whose childhood and adolescence unfolded in quite an unusual environment. I met him when he was eighteen years old and I found myself wondering what he would be like had he grown up in different family circumstances.

Wilson's parents married when in their mid-twenties. They had another son, two years younger than Wilson. Mr W owned a builder's firm and Mrs W was a secretary in a legal firm. When Wilson was nine years old, Mrs W started a relationship with another man, which led Mr W to move out of the house. Over the next several years Wilson and his brother moved between the father's and the mother's houses. But Mrs W developed serious psychological symptoms and it is interesting to learn how Wilson told me about this. "She has had good therapeutic help and she has gained in confidence: she used to answer any question with 'ask my husband', but she is now able to give her own answer".

After the parents' divorce, Wilson developed asthma and was put on very high doses of steroids, which severely affected his growth. As adolescence progressed, Wilson found himself struggling with sexual identity conflicts. He was, however, very successful intellectually and socially. Both his parents seemed to consider him "special" and often told him of their personal feelings and conflicts. He was captain of his year at school and much as with his parents, he found that colleagues, teachers, and even school staff would approach him to share their problems with him. Strikingly, he never lost his temper, always able to remain calm. At this point of his account I smiled and asked whether he was planning to become a politician. Wilson burst out laughing: "how could you guess? Yes, I am an active member of the Liberal party".

Wilson knew he needed help and he was very pleased when I gave him the address of a colleague who might see him. But he wanted to know where psychotherapy would lead. And "have you seen other youngsters who felt as I do?" I felt I wanted to respect his intellectual interest. I told him that the steroids would have played havoc with his hormones and I called his attention to the fact that his problems over sexual identity had started just at the time of his parents' divorce. Presumably, his understanding of what it meant to be "male" and what was "female", would have been affected. But I stressed how strongly it had impressed me in his account the extent to which both his parents had confided in him regarding their conflicts. After a brief pause, Wilson managed to mutter "It's not fair …" while tears came out of his eyes.

It is unfortunate and frustrating not to know how Wilson progressed into adulthood, but I am certain that he proved to be very successful at whatever career he decided to follow. This opinion results from my belief that Wilson felt "entitled" to activate his intellectual potentials. It is more difficult to hazard a guess over his capacity to move away from both parents and form his own family. I can only hope that he did go into psychotherapy and this helped him to cut or reduce his closeness to his parents.

Carlos

This was a man I met when working in the emergency department of a Casualty Hospital in Brazil. I was in my last year of medical school and doing shifts as an auxiliary anaesthetist. But I was keen to practise my clinical skills, so that when not in theatre, I was checking in and taking histories of the people who came in for help. This would eventually lead to my meeting a senior colleague, to whom I conveyed my findings, i.e., depending on how much they trusted my report, they went on to further enquiries and tests or simply issued a decision on how to proceed.

One day a man in his forties was admitted and clinical examination by other doctors found a rigid abdomen and because no significant data emerged from detailed questions, the decision followed to perform an exploratory laparotomy. I was told I would give him the general anaesthetic and, as usual, I went to the patient to introduce myself and enquire about any concurrent physical problems. I embarked on the usual questions about family, work, social life, and he gave me quiet, polite answers. Carlos was clearly a poor man who lived on his own and earned his living doing menial jobs. But after some ten minutes of our conversation, he stopped and made it clear that he wanted to tell me something important that was not covered by my routine questions. I indicated my agreement and, clearly hurt and ashamed, hesitating in his choice of words, he told me that the real reason for his coming to the hospital was that he had been masturbating himself anally with a bottle—and had suddenly pushed it in too hard, giving rise to sudden, terrible pain. He gave me permission to pass this information to the surgeons.

There was no longer a question of an "exploratory" laparotomy. The surgeons now knew exactly where to do the laparotomy. But this case left me with the question of what exactly had Carlos found in my approach that enabled him to reveal his secret.

Tony

A General Practitioner once asked me to see a boy of nine because of persistent abdominal pain. He had prescribed 150 mg of Ranitidine at night, since symptoms were worse after the boy went to bed, but as there was no improvement, he suggested consulting me before embarking on laboratory investigations. I saw Tony together with his parents. They told me of the family history and the boy spoke of his life at school and at home. Parents were successful professionals and my patient had two younger siblings. Gradually, a picture emerged of Tony going to bed and soon calling for help, demanding that a parent should lie beside him, always complaining of intense tummy pains. Quite often, he also woke up in the night, speaking of frightening nightmares and more abdominal pains. When I asked Tony to tell me some details about the nightmares, surprisingly he pointed to father and said, "it's *his* fault!" He went on to tell us the plot of *Congo* a horror film that, apparently besides other gory details, showed a gorilla opening a man's chest and throwing the lungs at the screen.

Both parents were shocked at this account and I noticed how they exchanged reproachful looks. After a pause, mother mentioned that father was "addicted" to horror films and, rather embarrassed, they admitted that Tony often stayed with his father watching these films. After a strained pause, the father asked Tony "Is that when you get your tummy pains?" Tony meekly answered: "Yes …" After a heavy pause, I asked him "So, how do you know when it is pain and when it is fear?" Tony looked very lost—"I don't know, really …" Two weeks later the parents contacted me and said that, following our meeting, Tony was no longer allowed to watch the horror movies and, predictably, the night-time pains and panics had ceased.

This case shows how difficult it can be for the child and the parents to find the words that will allow them to understand each other. Tony's parents managed to calm him down when he complained of nightmares, but when his reporting "tummy pains" led to repeated visits to the GP: it is possible that Tony sensed that pain elicited a "more caring" response from the parents. As our meeting unfolded, this link became increasingly clear until Tony's father could ask him the crucial question that led to the boy's recognition that he had not been able to differentiate between the two kinds of distress. As soon as this was put into words, Tony and his parents were able to break the vicious circle of his symptoms. The unconscious fantasies underlying Tony's pathological behaviour were not identified and articulated, but however surprising this might seem to psychotherapy practitioners, it is a finding that I have come to consider almost predictable. If the professional *understands* the pathogenic unconscious fantasy, it is not so important the manner in which he utilises this knowledge—somehow, the child grasps it. In the family context, as soon as the parents are able to appreciate the child's anxieties and manage to modify their approach to the child, the symptoms disappear.

John

This lawyer was in his early fifties when he came to see me. He found himself in a situation where a decision might solve quite a number of his problems, but he was not managing to implement any definite changes. He had been married for over twenty years and had a son and a daughter, both leading successful academic and social lives. He had a brother five years younger than him who had been born with an I.Q. in the low thirties.

John married Julia and soon found they clashed over the issue of having children: he did not want to have any, but Julia was adamant that they should have them. He eventually agreed to this and they went on to have two sons. Somehow, after the birth of the younger child, they stopped their sexual life. Eventually, a new complication arose: John became attracted to a colleague and, much to his surprise, this lady visited his home and became friendly with Julia. Serious and complex changes developed in the marital relationship between John and Julia. Before long, Julia began to demand a divorce—while John was not so convinced that he wanted to marry his lover or that she would ever want to marry him. Listening to John's account, I felt quite convinced that this lady was only aiming at tormenting him. Julia seemed prepared to give him time to decide what he wanted to do, but the other lady kept pushing him away and then trying to seduce him back.

So we came to one session where John was recounting and debating what he obviously experienced as torture. And at one point he said: "This is not right ... it's too destructive!" I decided to ask, "What is, what constitutes destructiveness?" And even if his profession involved a deep involvement with language, he could not articulate the obvious fact that his lover was being destructive. I decided to put it to him that my guess was that from a very young age, he had been led to see destructiveness *not* as a condemnable thing, but something that had to be tolerated—I had in mind, and I mentioned it, his younger brother's intellectual limitations and my assumption that John's parents had learnt to show an attitude of understanding and forgiveness, that is, that his younger brother could not behave differently. John's eyes filled with tears and he struggled to tell me how the boy would tear up books, smash toys and games—and if John dared to protest, it was he who was punished by the parents.

After a couple of weeks, John managed to tell his lover to move out of the J's home and he worked hard at not responding to her attempts to make contact again. It took some three months before his relationship with Julia was restored to a more harmonious, mutually satisfying condition.

I find this case a dramatic example of how important it is for the analyst to "recognise" a significant word or sentence that represents the lid of a Pandora's box. Unfortunately, this is not a step that can be taught. Empathy is vital and intuition becomes a tool that can be acted upon to meet the overt manifestation of the patient's unconscious wish to convey the nature of a painful feeling. In other words, I tend to underline the importance of "asking the right questions".

Moses

This gentleman was in his early fifties when he came to see me. He came in a luxurious chauffeur-driven car and phoned me about half an hour before our arranged time, asking if I could see him then. I was able to do so and he came in to my consulting room.

Moses had seen a couple of psychotherapists and he told me about these experiences. He saw the first one for nearly fifteen years; first once, then twice, and later three times per week. He told me that he stopped when he became tired of hearing his therapist telling him of his family problems. Somehow, what followed with the second therapist was not too different.

Moses was a successful businessman. He had complaints about his wife, but they had managed to bring up their three children and led a reasonably harmonious life, even though sex had ceased to be part of their relationship for several years and Moses managed to indicate to me that plenty of conflicts were swept under the carpet. His wife also consulted another psychotherapist. Moses told me of his earlier life. He adored his father and described his mother as "awful", hence his hating her. In fact, his father had had similar feelings and had divorced his wife, proceeding some time later to marry a woman many years younger than himself.

When Moses told me about his children and it emerged that his daughter was struggling with a nervous breakdown, I said that he certainly had many family problems to cope with. He smiled and said: "You know? Work is the only thing that turns me on!" So, what kept him from seeking some change? He shrugged his shoulders and said words similar to the dictum that the devil you know is better than the devil you do not know.

We were coming to the end of our consultation and I could not avoid my impression that the feelings Moses had expressed about his family were almost certainly duplicated in the matter of therapists. In other words, rather than coming to see me, he would prefer to see one of the therapists he had already met. He found words that, in a very diplomatic way, confirmed my impression, but it was his summing-up of our meeting that led me to describe this story: "I must confess that listening to you, chatting here, I feel there are doors that might get open—and I am not sure that I really want that ..."

He was surprised at my fees, claiming he had always paid much less than that amount, but still gave me a cheque and we agreed that he would get in touch if he wanted to see me again. Indeed, Moses did not contact me again.

Regina

I only met this young Polish lady a few times, since she was always travelling to other European countries. Regina's is probably the most unusual story I met in my consulting room. She was in her late twenties when she came to see me at the recommendation of a GP who did not really know how best to help her. Regina had trouble sleeping and was lately experiencing dizzy spells, as well as feeling sick after meals.

Regina's mother worked as a secretary. She hated men and taught Regina to be wary of them saying things like "if a man does not like his mother, that is how he will treat you." Her mother had never been married and when a boyfriend suddenly broke off their relationship, she decided to have a child—and she turned to what she called "a live sperm bank", a neighbour who, she knew, had fathered children by several women. Regina was eleven years old when her mother formed a relationship with a man who adopted Regina and developed a very loving, protective relationship with her.

Regina became pregnant when having sex with her first boyfriend, but having terminated this, she again fell pregnant eighteen months later from a new boyfriend. Second termination ... Regina tried to concentrate on her education, coming to England and joining a very good College to learn about nutrition. At one point a colleague introduced her to web-stripping and Regina soon discovered that "being a call girl gave me better money—I only worked five days per month and this gave me enough money for my expenses". And it was on one of these days that she met her present boyfriend: he was English, had been married and had two children with whom he kept in close contact. He also introduced her to Internet skills.

Regina was delighted to find that this man's family accepted her warmly, but she told me of her surprise to find that they fought among themselves "all the time". Gradually, another side of the picture emerged: this man was possessive, wanted her to be available at all times and keep away from her friends. Worse, he had a best friend with whom he went out drinking, promptly getting drunk and when they came back to the flat where they now lived, he demanded Regina should move away to another room. To her surprise, she became pregnant ... she decided to have a termination and wanted to do it in Poland, to be near her mother. He opposed this and she gave in, having the intervention here—and the next day he was out, drinking with friends and ignoring her. She could not forgive him, but neither was she able to move away. I gave her my interpretation of her type of indecision/helplessness, saying that she felt life was giving her better prospects than those her mother had struggled with—and urged her to have long-term therapy.

Regina left London to visit her mother and later sent me a message—she did manage to move away from this boyfriend and intended to pursue her skills in communication techniques. Yes, she agreed she should have therapy and she would seek this in the near future. But I had no further news from Regina.

Hilde

I only saw this lady once, but I want to describe her story because it was one of the most dramatic examples of what might be considered running away from one's shadow. Hilde was in her mid-thirties when we met. Strikingly attractive and appearing much younger than her age, she had had many years of five times per week analysis until a couple of years before contacting me. She was a very successful academic and had published many books in her field. She was married to a very senior banker, whom she described as peaceful and sociable. He had been married to "a quite crazy" lady and had two teenage daughters from that marriage.

Hilde had married this man when the children were toddlers. Since coming to live in London, the couple were having a tormented life. The older daughter registered in a college, but stayed in bed most of the day—and when Hilde tried to encourage her to work properly, her father told Hilde it was not for her to intervene. She felt hurt and protested, which led him to spend many days without speaking to her. But beyond this, he was now refusing to go out or to meet people.

Hilde was afraid of the relationship coming to an end, since she thought she might be moving from "safety" to "insecurity". She saw my expression of surprise and decided to tell me that her husband had left all his possessions for his first wife and that his work salary was a secret: every month he made a deposit of some money in her bank account and this was all.

Hilde's father had been a military officer who had "destroyed my mother": he was "a terrible man and she is just too weak". Hilde's younger sister had been married for five years and had no children. Hilde had gone through two terminations earlier in her life and a third one soon after getting married. "My husband wants another child, but I never wanted one". She added that getting older, she was now wondering whether she should, might or wanted to become a mother.

Hilde told me of having gone through several affairs, including one man who wanted to marry her, but "I did not want to leave my husband." Well, what about the sexual side of the marriage? "Oh, well … we have not had sex for quite a long time …" was her answer.

Hilde seemed to feel happy with our meeting and said she wanted to start regular psychotherapy. But having made an appointment for a further session, she telephoned me hours before the arranged time and told me she had to travel abroad. She would contact me on her return—but she never did. After a couple of weeks, I sent her a letter offering a new meeting, but Hilde replied that she was not sure about her timetable.

Indeed one might consider that Hilde felt that her academic success was "enough, sufficient" achievement, but I thought that her descriptions of relationships made it very clear that she felt lonely, undervalued, and deprived of fulfilling her capacities as a woman who might become a mother. Unfortunately, only further therapy might help me to understand why Hilde could not gain the benefits of her abilities and, hopefully, enable her to achieve this.

Jeremy

This was a very painful consultation I had many years ago. Jeremy was a charming, incredibly articulate, and intelligent eight-year-old boy. His parents had divorced two years earlier, though they had been living apart for four to five years. It was the boy's school that called in the parents, warning them of the fact that Jeremy was clearly a very unhappy boy who needed help. The parents embarked on a typical conflict, regarding which route to follow in search of that help and indeed they obtained many diverging recommendations. Somehow they came to see me.

Jeremy was brought to my consulting room by both parents. They wanted first to see me on their own and Jeremy agreed to wait in an adjoining room, where he did make a couple of drawings that he was happy to show and describe to me: essentially they showed a villain stabbing a poor, charming man. But while I was speaking to his parents, I could see through a little gap in my consulting room sliding doors that Jeremy was coming and staying there for several minutes before moving back to the other room.

The parents told me about their life together and about their families of origin. Their accounts can be reported, but not everyone would really manage to make sense of the conflicts implied in their stories. They were both Jewish, but one of them came from an Ashkenazy family, while the other came from a Sephardi family. Sending Jeremy to a Jewish school was mandatory, but which orientation? And whose opinion should prevail? Parents alone? Oh, no. Grandparents were also involved and demanded Jeremy be sent to their chosen school. After a while, being Jewish myself, I did not know whether to show surprise and horror or, instead, just laugh at a picture that, however painful, had a touch of the ridiculous. But even if one managed to ignore the words, it was still shocking to watch the amount of anger and fear that the couple were showing.

The parents did agree that I should see Jeremy by himself. This was when he explained to me the contents of his drawings and I was shocked to learn that these were not just something he might have seen on TV or something similar. Jeremy was afraid, perhaps even convinced, that his maternal grandfather was determined to kill his father. And I was certain that Jeremy was telling me of feelings he was aware of most of his waking life. Jeremy's description of his life seemed exaggerated, but he told me of a sense of isolation that one does not wish on anyone, let alone a child. "They are always busy! They never hear what I say, nor do they want to know it either. Only the au pair takes or picks me up from school, but she doesn't want to know anything, either. They cannot stop fighting each other!" But the worse, or the bit that most frightened Jeremy was his conviction that "Grandpa" was determined to kill his father.

What we, outsiders, might find surprising and touching, was Jeremy's formulation of what the future might bring: "If he killed my mother, I would be looked after by her family that is very large, but if he killed my father, I would be an orphan! I don't want to be an orphan!"

I told the parents that they should consider marital therapy and urged them to place Jeremy in regular psychotherapy. We did agree on a follow-up meeting, but not surprisingly, they cancelled it. And what could I do to help this lovely, suffering boy?

Cecily

I saw this thirty-four-year-old lady for a consultation following her application to a training society for a psychotherapy vacancy, which unfortunately means I am unable to present a follow-up to our meeting. I decided to describe my findings here because she was one of the most resilient people I have met. In spite of her life-long traumatic experiences, Cecily managed to pursue her studies and her work, achieving positions of seniority in very reputable companies.

Cecily's mother had her first child in her early teens and was forced to give that child up for adoption. She was involved with an Eastern man when she became pregnant with Cecily, but she never agreed to give Cecily any information about her father. Not long after Cecily's birth, her mother gave birth to another child from an African father—another relationship that broke down after a short time. A few years later she married a Caribbean gentleman, with whom she gave birth to two more children.

Cecily was a tall, thin, very attractive lady. Among her siblings, she had the lightest coloured skin; though not "quite white", she would never stand out in a crowd because of her appearance (colour-wise). Cecily had been living on and off with the same gentleman since her early twenties. At one point she had a brief affair with another man and became pregnant, but not being sure of whose child that was, she decided on a termination. In her mid-twenties Cecily gave birth to a daughter and two years later she fell pregnant again, but this time tragedy hit her: scans revealed the foetus had died and surgery was required to remove it.

Sadly, the old saying that the lightning never strikes the same place twice proved wrong and when Cecily became pregnant again it was found that she was carrying twins—but scans indicated some pathology. Absolute torture followed with gynaecologists and obstetricians suggesting how to proceed and Cecily struggling to balance their varying recommendations and her wish to give birth to normal babies. Eventually, Caesarean section brought two normal babies into the world and after some weeks under observation in hospital, they were discharged. What I felt brought a light touch to the picture was Cecily's insistence on breast-feeding the babies for nine months—a decision that led relatives and friends to "chastise" her for "delaying" the babies' normal diet.

It all sounded to me as a very eventful life with plenty of conflicts and traumas. But if I admired Cecily's resilience, resourcefulness, and determination, she felt that she had potentials she had not developed properly—hence her wish to have therapy. I had no doubt that Cecily would prove to be a "successful patient" and recommended she should be offered a vacancy.

Manoel

I first saw this Brazilian boy when he was seven years old. Immensely bright and articulate, his parents asked for help because he kept banging his head on his bed or the wall by the bed. Manoel had an older brother, with whom he got on quite well, though occasionally getting into fights. He had a good circle of friends and was very successful in his school life. When in my consulting room, he quickly made himself comfortable, admiring pictures and decorations, occasionally asking me for information about their origin.

Manoel's parents were senior professionals. They came from middle class families and their answers about their backgrounds brought forward no significant datum. They were happy to allow their son to answer my questions, never correcting him. When I asked the boy what led him to bang his head, he told me that he had dreams where a "crioulo" (black man) appeared and tried to force-feed him. Apparently, the "crioulo" tried to feed him vomit and this led him to wake up-and Manoel was convinced that he banged his head to get rid of the dream. His parents smiled as if they had already heard this explanation, but made no comments. I asked him when did these nightmares start? "Inside my Mummy's tummy." I asked if only the "crioulo" appeared, and he answered, "No, the 'crioulinha' (little black lady) is also there, though not all the time".

I sincerely believe that the way things turned out was not "a result" of my involvement: Manoel stopped banging his head … He was relieved, his parents were happy and we waited for developments. Some months later the banging started again, but luckily they ceased after another consultation. Two years later I was approached again and this time Manoel gave a different explanation to his head banging: this was to call his parents when he woke up from some dream. But, his parents asked, why not come to our room and call us? And his answer: "I don't like to walk in the dark corridor—and you have also told me that I was forbidden from going to your bedroom!" His parents jumped—"We never said anything like that!" and Manoel replied, "yes, you did say it last year!"

Manoel improved again and I lost touch with the family. But, contrary to most (if not all!) of my cases, I have had news of his progress. Now in his adolescence what is Manoel doing? He is a successful musician, having won a prestigious scholarship to a prominent foreign musical College!

Would anyone be able to guess where adolescence would take the child Manoel? Indeed, would any of his music teachers ever guess what "problems" Manoel had as a child? I hope I can be forgiven for my black-humour comment that "banging his head" may well have been an early indication of Manoel's awareness of sound and rhythm—a predecessor of his later studies. If only all children could achieve a similar positive development of their early pathological symptoms!

Viviane

This lady was in her late thirties when she came to see me for a consultation. She told me she was "not yet ready" to have therapy, but she hoped I could give her some advice about problems she was experiencing. Her parents had been born in different countries and the family had moved round several countries. Viviane herself had found a job in the banking world that also involved a great deal of travelling. I thought of describing our meeting because, to my surprise, she gave me a variation I had never known on an old theme.

Viviane had a couple of long-term relationships and she married her husband when she was in her late twenties. Neither of them wanted to have children, but in her mid-thirties Viviane asked him to give her this present. Their sexual encounters had always been quite infrequent and, very reluctantly, her husband agreed to her request—and she gave birth to a son, who was developing quite normally.

But Viviane told me of a different kind of problem. On a couple of occasions her husband had attacked her and when this happened again, she called for the Police. Eventually, this crisis was sorted out and she agreed he should live again in their house. But he now became verbally aggressive and Viviane was contemplating a divorce. And this was the subject on which she wanted advice.

We discussed Viviane's feelings and impulses. She had recently been diagnosed as having a serious illness that would require complex treatment and this made her feel vulnerable. But she desperately wanted to free herself from her husband. Eventually our discussion led to the obvious question: "Has your husband been threatening you?" And it was her answer that justified this account: "No …" and after a pause, "But he did say he is considering suicide …"

I tried to share Viviane's sense of powerlessness—whatever she did would not guarantee a better life for either herself or her husband. But considering the issue of "violence" in this couple's life, I thought that a threat of suicide was quite an unusual expression of hostility or aggression. I offered to see Viviane again, but she was soon travelling abroad and, contrary to my expectation, did not contact me on her return to London.

Raphael

I am including this account in the chapter on "Unusual stories", but unfortunately what I found is not so rare or uncommon. What is certainly very unusual is for parents like the Rs to consult a professional; in fact, I could not find any similar cases in the files of my private practice, though I did see quite a few people similar to the Rs in my NHS work. They would come to my clinic because of this being demanded by teachers or Social Services: and they would stress that they were coming against their will.

A colleague of mine worked as a psychologist at a top private primary school and the teachers asked him to see Raphael, a nine-year-old who was very unhappy and often crying, complaining of being ignored or bullied by other children. After seeing Raphael and his parents, my colleague suggested to them that they might find it helpful to consult me and discuss whether Raphael would benefit from psychotherapy.

Mr R was Australian and worked in the London branch of an international bank. His mother had suffered from colon cancer and went through painful and mostly ineffective treatments, finally dying not long before his coming to see me. He had to deal with all the practical details of her death and only "after a while" did he find himself mourning her loss, "but mainly when on my own".

Mrs R was Irish and a senior barrister. It turned out that her mother had also died of cancer (of the breast), having surgery and chemotherapy, all to no effect. From her tone of voice, stating facts rather drily, I ended up with the impression that Mrs R had never grieved the loss of her mother, however competently dealing with the resulting practicalities and professional demands.

Both Mr and Mrs R were in their early forties. They had met in London many years earlier and soon decided to get married. They were in full agreement that neither of them wanted to have children, but as they found themselves moving through their thirties, they thought that, who knows? Perhaps it would be good to have a child? This is how Raphael came to be born, and a sister was born two years later.

But Mrs R went back to work when each child reached four months. Nannies looked after the children. Most of these nannies would leave after twelve to eighteen months, but substitutes were quickly found. As I now looked at Mr R he understood my expression, and went on to explain that his job never really allowed him to spend much time during the day at home—and most times, the children would be in bed when he got home.

And I made what apparently was a wrong step … I felt that I had to express to Mr and Mrs R what was my understanding of their son's emotional experiences and resulting complaints. I said that my impression was that Raphael was reacting to feelings of loss—not only the grandmothers passing away, but also unconsciously afraid that something might happen to his busy parents. Mrs R tried hard to be diplomatic, but her voice was pretty sharp: "oh, come on! You must know that children don't mind these things! They are terribly fickle!"

I should mention that I did ask Mrs R how she reacted to her mother's death and she asked her husband to tell me: "you never cried … I knew you were upset …" When I asked her if she knew that her husband had grieved for the loss of his mother "when on his own", she shrugged her shoulders, saying nothing explicitly.

I thought Mr and Mrs R were what I call "doers", active and productive, but not comfortable with feelings. I tried, however subtly, to call their attention to the fact that this emotional posture was bound to affect Raphael's sense of their availability. We finished our meeting with my suggesting I should see them together with Raphael again and they said they would think about it and let me know. But, not surprisingly, I never heard from them again.

Brenda

I only saw this thirty-six-year-old lady once. She must have understood from my comments that I did not believe I could help her—and she was correct.

Brenda was extremely tense, speaking at great speed and occasionally checking whether I was following her. She had a very thin body, but heavy legs and cheeks. She said she suffered from bulimia—only thinks of eating, while dreading the idea of getting fat, but then after going for days without eating breakfast or lunch, will wake up in the night and empty the fridge and shelves, eating for four to five hours non-stop. Because of this incapacity to control herself, Brenda had turned to medication and, perhaps predictably, become addicted to several drugs (thyroid, diuretics, laxatives).

Brenda was the youngest of six children. The eldest sister had died a few years earlier. Her father had been an active, rich supermarket owner, quiet, friendly, devoted to the children, and he had died when she was in her early twenties. Her mother was now in her seventies, but Brenda had little to say about her. As a child, Brenda had a strict Catholic upbringing and she felt hers had been a happy childhood.

In her teens, Brenda had a boyfriend; the relationship lasted for eight years, in spite of several separations; he was described as "very correct", that is, never touched her beyond gently kissing her. This young man wanted Brenda to marry him, but she was reluctant to do this. A few months before our meeting, she had met another man, several years younger than her and now she found herself struggling with unexpected problems. From weekend meetings, they moved on to more and more frequent ones and then he would spend the weekends at Brenda's flat. But, when having sex, she could not cope with his penetrating her: when he tried, she would lock her legs, terrified that she would feel pain, it would bleed and she moved away. Brenda agreed to masturbate him, but when ejaculation approached, she would take her hands away, dreading feeling disgusted by what would come out of the penis. He would occasionally touch her clitoris, but she claimed to feel nothing.

Brenda had spoken to friends about her problems and they usually mocked her, advising her to get pornographic magazines or watch similar films. She had consulted various specialists and tried alternative medicine—no results. And so we came to the crucial question: could I help her? I did not believe Brenda could deal with insight, but I said we might try a few meetings. I urged her to consult a couple of specialist colleagues who might help her with her digestive and gynaecological problems, but I do not think she ever contacted them. We made a tentative appointment, but not surprisingly Brenda phoned me a few days later to cancel this.

I have not been able to find reasonable hypotheses to explain Brenda's sexual problems. Our psychoanalytic literature offers endless theories to explain her obsession with food and self-image, but I could not find a convincing one that might explain her sexual anxieties. Perhaps long-term work might allow us to discover pathogenic experiences in Brenda's earlier life, but she was reluctant to try this out.

Noemi

A colleague asked me to see Noemi and at the end of our consultation she agreed that she should have therapy, but told me she would prefer to see a woman—whereupon I referred her to a colleague. I have no follow-up information on our meeting, but I am recounting it here because Noemi told me of an obsession she struggled with—and I had never met or heard of such a conflict.

Noemi was in her late teens. A good-looking and very intelligent girl she told me of her background and her present life. Her parents came from different countries and had formed a close, loving family with their four children. Noemi had always been very successful in her studies and had quite a few close friends. As a child, she worried about being overweight and later complained of "too heavy" periods. At the time when I saw her, Noemi had developed some food fads, but said this was "not important".

But she must have felt able to trust me, because she decided to tell me of an obsession that "only one other person knows about". She was unable to tolerate odd numbers and immediately felt compelled to transform them into even ones. Noemi gave me an example: "if I see twenty-seven, I quickly turn it into two times seven equals fourteen." How could I respond to this information? I tried not to smile and, after a pause I reminded her that when speaking of her maternal grandmother, she had mentioned that "she is an evil eye"—that is, not "has evil eyes", but only one. Was that an example that upset her? She denied this was significant.

Christiana

This lady was not sure that she wanted to engage in therapy, but she decided to follow a friend's advice and came to see me. We had such a painful meeting that I assumed I had gained her confidence and that she would see me again—but this did not happen. Having made a second appointment, Christiana cancelled it, saying she had to travel to her home country to visit a relative. And I did not hear from her again.

When seeing a new patient for a consultation interview, I allocate one and a half to two hours for the meeting. Christiana's interview went on to a bit more than ninety minutes and I believe that never have I met a person who had lived through such dramatic and traumatic experiences. Christiana was born in Sweden, where her family still lived. She was just over forty years old when we met and she had a younger sister, married with three children.

Christiana was a successful architect and had been living in London since her early twenties. She told me of her relationship with a Jewish young man that lasted for five years, when he finally felt forced to admit that he would not manage to go against his family's opposition to his getting married to a gentile lady. She then met Julius, a senior barrister who insisted she must marry him, since he felt she was the woman he had been looking for all his life. One problem though: he did not want to have children. They had managed to establish a *modus vivendi*, where he never slept more than two or three hours each night, which seemed to explain his continuous state of tension and frequent emotional outbursts. But Christiana saw her age advancing and she was desperately keen to have a child. Surprisingly, Julius agreed she should have IVF and, luckily, she gave birth to a very healthy boy. And very gratifyingly, Christiana found that Julius wanted to bring up this boy as his own child. Happy? Indeed. Christiana felt life moving in a positive direction when one night she woke up and, looking for Julius she found that he had hung himself from a rope he had tied to a high banister. He had left no messages that might explain his action. Christiana was shocked; she felt guilty, convinced that it was her decision to have a child that had triggered Julius' suicide.

It took many months for Christiana to recover. Then having dinner with friends, she met Serge and "immediately we felt that we had been made for each other". After some further meetings they moved to live together and Christiana was relieved and delighted that Serge got on very well with her son. But, much to her horror, after no more than one year, one night Serge woke up feeling breathless and only minutes later he died in the arms of Christiana. He had suffered a ruptured aortic aneurism.

Well, one would imagine that if there was a God, he would think Christiana had suffered enough pain. Sadly, this was not the case. After Serge's death she decided to spend some time with her family and then just over two months later her father died!

I hope Christiana found some happier experiences after going through such traumatic losses.

Mr Maxwell

This gentleman was in his mid-forties when he came to see me. He was having problems with his lady partner and was seeking help to reach a decision about how to proceed. A successful professional, he had devoted himself to various enterprises, invariably moving on after a few years. He had had several long-term relationships and was now living with a lady friend, whom he had met eight years before consulting me. He described himself as having a low sexual drive and he was aware of the role this had played in his relationships. Apparently his "low sexual drive" only played a role in his involvement with his partners—masturbation was frequent and gratifying, but only practised when he was on his own.

We discussed his early history, but I could not identify any datum that might explain the conflicts he was now facing. His siblings had also faced difficulties in their adult lives, but Mr Maxwell had an image of his parents as "normal middle-middle class people", with no distinguishing features. He had consulted many doctors and therapists over the years, seeking help for his sense of frustration and unhappiness. He had taken anti-depressive medication, with only minimal improvement. His account of his psychotherapy sessions before coming to see me were quite surprising and unusual. According to Mr Maxwell, his therapist would always answer telephone calls during his sessions, explaining that "real life has to go on". There were times when he would interrupt the session to take his own blood pressure and, incredibly, quite a few times the therapist cut the session short "because he had to see his doctor, who was worried about his blood pressure". I had never heard such reports about the style of my colleagues' work. This account could not but lead to my question: why did Mr Maxwell continue to see this gentleman? "Well … at other times I had really found him helpful …"

Mr Maxwell found himself now facing conflicts in the relationship with his partner. They had repeated confrontations because of his partner's requests, demands for a sexual involvement from him—much as with his therapist, Mr Maxwell felt ignored and subject to the selfish interests of the person with whom he was involved. Why continue the relationship? As with his therapist, he valued the partnership because quite often he found his lady-friend helpful and loveable.

Mr Maxwell moved away from London after a few months of therapy. I was left feeling frustrated because I had not managed to find the reasons why this mature, intelligent, and most competent gentleman was unable to discover any other outlets to his sexual drive than his compulsive masturbation—while sustaining relationships with partners he saw as selfish and frustrating.

CHAPTER FOUR

Interesting stories

The following accounts describe events that happened in the course of some patients' lives. Their occurrence had no particular, obvious links with that person's ordinary life, though their earlier experiences clearly influenced the manner in which they reacted to the specific episodes related here.

Julius

It was many years ago that Julius came to see me for psychoanalysis. He was twenty-one years old and coming to the end of his medical training. A brilliant student, he had always achieved considerable academic success and had a large circle of friends. Intelligent and articulate, he could handle most adequately his social life. But the preceding two years of his life had brought much unhappiness: he had fallen in love with a girl whose origin led his parents to oppose their relationship.

Julius was the firstborn son and he had grown up aware of the extent to which parents and grandparents saw him as their dearest child. They were not strict practitioners of their religion, but this still represented an important element in their lives. Julius was well aware of their feelings and he only brought his girlfriend to the house after months of going out with her. Sadly, his worst forebodings were confirmed; the parents praised the girl's qualities, but could not conceive of her joining the family.

We embarked on our therapy and each session was filled with painful accounts of endless episodes where Julius had clashed with one or the other of his parents. He would speak about his medical placements and meetings with friends and colleagues, but the main *leitmotiv* was the girlfriend and his agonising conflict of loyalties: he didn't want to hurt his parents, but he loved his girlfriend and didn't want to lose her either.

After some weeks of analysis, Julius recounted what was his first dream since starting therapy. He dreamt that he was celebrating his marriage to his girlfriend. Friends, colleagues, family, lots of people had come to the ceremony and there was universal joy. After the religious rituals had been performed, the young couple went down the aisle and as they got near the door, Julius felt some uncomfortable itch in his ear and could not resist putting his finger there. To his surprise, he had brought out a little ball of wax, which made him feel quite embarrassed. The dream finished soon after that.

In line with the "correct technique" of inviting the patient to free associate to the dream, I asked him what the various events of the dream had meant to him. He voiced his disbelief and pain at the thought that only in a dream could he imagine his longings coming true. He made one or two comments about some people in the dream and then focused on the "ball of wax". He smiled and told me that only the preceding morning he had attended a lesson at the Pathology department and he remembered looking at a bottle containing a specimen of a brain tumour: its shape and colour reminded him of the "ball of wax" in the dream.

The only comment that I felt justified in making about this dream was much the same as Julius himself had made, that is, the dream depicted the fulfilment of a desperate wish—which confirmed one of the main assertions Freud had made about dreams.

After a few further months of therapy, Julius complained of a recurrent headache. I used to see him early in the mornings and Julius himself attributed the headache to nights where he had slept little and badly. I found some more complex possibilities to link the headache to his emotional pain, but his complaints continued. After some weeks, he decided to consult the medical services attached to his university. He told me that the physician had considered the headache "psychosomatic" and encouraged him to continue with his analysis, while resorting to various analgesics. We plodded on.

But the headaches did not disappear. They were not continuous, but appeared quite often. After a few more weeks, I encouraged Julius to look for a second opinion. In those days, the split between private and NHS facilities was not as dramatic as it has become in our days, but Julius would never consider using his father's money to gain access to private doctors. He sought the same student services, but this time the consultant who saw him took a different view of the situation: he referred Julius for further tests and for a neurological consultation. Julius informed me of this by telephone; he had to cancel his next session because the neurologist was due to see him the next day. And what followed took place very quickly, indeed. X-rays and other tests confirmed the doctors' clinical impression of a brain tumour. An exploratory surgical intervention left Julius virtually comatose and he died a few days later.

When I met one of my senior medical analyst colleagues, I was very shaken. This was not just "another patient". He was someone I liked as a person and his being a medical student brought in that dreaded dimension of "there, but for the grace of God, go I". My senior colleague reminded me that it was part of a doctor's life to have a patient dying, whatever the treatment he had been receiving. As we came to discuss the months of therapy, I brought up the contents of Julius' first dream. Could this be seen as evidence of some unconscious awareness of a diseased body? As true believers in the psyche-soma unit, surely we had to consider this possibility?

My senior colleague was Michael Balint, an eminent psychoanalyst who pioneered analytic work with groups of general practitioners. Psychosomatics was very much a speciality of his. But he laughed, a typical open, warm laughter, and said, kindly, but firmly, that I could feel free to take the dream as evidence of that "awareness", but sadly, he added, how would it help me if and when I found another patient who reported a dream with similar features? Would I really automatically refer my analytic patient for neurological screening?

I was disappointed, and my puzzlement remained alive to this day. The ironic final touch of this story came with the pathologist's report on Julius' tumour: he had been presented with a clinical history stating that headaches had been present for *some weeks or a few months, with no other symptoms*. But in his report the pathologist said he had found areas of the tumour showing changes that indicated the tumour had been present for *many* months.

Graham

Back in the seventies I was working in a Child Guidance Clinic and one day the local Comprehensive school's educational psychologist referred a young sixteen-year-old, Graham, for a consultation. His teachers had decided to expel him, as they found his behaviour totally unacceptable.

Graham came to the interview with his older stepsister, who was in charge of his upbringing. A detailed discussion of the boy's history and his present situation at school and at home left me with no doubt that he was not a behaviourally disturbed young man. He admitted to a number of pranks, mostly engaged in when with other peers, but his view of teachers and adults in general showed considerable sensitivity and concern for the feelings of others. I eventually concluded that the teachers' appraisal of Graham was not impartial, but probably influenced by the fact of his being black.

It happened that I had recently made contact with the headmaster of a highly rated central London school, also ran by the Educational Authorities, but offering a much higher level of academic studies than Graham's present Comprehensive school. I had been impressed by the liberal, warm views of this headmaster and I hoped he would be prepared to offer an assessment interview to my patient. Fortunately, he did accept my request. He interviewed Graham and proceeded to offer him a place at the school. Graham made a very successful career at the school and, subsequently, at university. From a "nasty, troublesome black boy", he had become another success story in a very good school.

Patrick J.

I was interviewing Mr and Mrs J, to discuss their concern over their son, Patrick's, reluctance to join in with parents and siblings in their daily activities. Especially Mr J felt himself disrespected and ignored by Patrick. At one point of our meeting, he remembered a story: "When Patrick was four years old, he came to me one day and said '*I know* it was God who created the Earth!' I said this was good. He then insisted

'Do you want me to tell you how it is I know?' I said 'yes' and he explained: 'because there was no ground for anyone to stand on, so only a God could have done it'".

I could not refrain from smiling. Throughout our conversation I had been searching for clues that might explain Patrick's detachment, distance from his father. Suddenly, Mr J's account seemed to contain that rationale I had been looking for: when he mentioned that he had replied to Patrick's question with a cool "I said this was good", I became certain that Patrick took these words as dismissive, hence his emphatic question "do you *want* to know?"

Mr J was taken aback when I suggested to him that this episode had probably remained in Patrick's memory as evidence of Mr J's lack of interest in what he wanted to say to him—hence his presently "ignoring" Mr J.

I happened to meet Mrs J a few months later and she told me that her husband had made cautious but definite attempts to come closer to Patrick and this had actually improved their relationship.

Roberto

This young man was in his late twenties when he contacted me because of a severe panic crisis that reduced him to frequent crying episodes and made it impossible for him to carry out his work commitments. He was a very successful IT specialist, who had developed his own consultancy firm since arriving in the UK. After telling me about his symptoms, we discussed his history. His parents had different nationalities and were very successful in their professions. Roberto had two older sisters: one ten and the other twelve years older than him. Both were married and lived happily in Spain, where all three had been born. I noticed that Roberto seemed particularly stirred emotionally when telling me about his sisters, but I gave no particular significance to this at the time he told me about it.

After a number of short relationships, Roberto became attached to a young man who was several years younger than him. He told me he was deeply in love with this "boy", seeing himself as supporting, protecting, nursing, looking after him. One day, this young man decided to break off their relationship and Roberto went to pieces. Long arguments, painful pleas and the lover relented. They went on holiday together, but coming back to London they soon started to face disagreements and anxieties. Eventually the lover decided to go abroad for a couple of weeks, to "cool off".

Roberto felt lonely and anxious, praying that his lover would come back and resume their close relationship. But the day before he was due to return to London, the young man sent Roberto a message, informing him that he was not coming back to London—and Roberto fell to pieces. He resorted to no sleep, no food, writing endless letters about his feelings, phoning all members of his family, non-stop.

We discussed these feelings from various angles. Roberto sincerely believed that his lover needed his protection, but he could admit that he was the one who was feeling not just abandoned, but also unprotected. His feelings of resentment were enmeshed with the pain of feeling betrayed.

I had met people in similar conflicts and had found that many times these "unique, incomparably painful" experiences can in fact result from an old wound being brought to the surface again. I said to Roberto that he clearly felt betrayed and asked him to concentrate on that precise moment when he had received his lover's last message: did it ring any bells? Had he ever "been there" before? No, he answered, he could not remember anything like that, definitely not. After a brief pause, I explained that I had never seen such a powerful reaction as he had described to me, except when it was happening "again"—and I went on to mention my earlier impression of how his face had become illuminated when he told me how much he had loved one of his sisters.

Roberto jumped: "Stop there! I can't believe it! How could you get that? When I was eleven years old my parents took me away from our home town, moving to the North, leaving my sisters behind. I cried and could not stop crying: I cried on the plane and I cried for weeks! I can see it now—this guy has taken my sisters' place!" His excitement abated and tears now flowed from his eyes.

Our sessions continued for some months. Roberto felt he had overcome the loss of his lover and he now felt freer to enjoy his social and professional life.

This "have you been there before?" question appears in several of the cases described in this book. I have met quite a few people struggling with very painful experiences, who kept putting forward interpretations for their pain, while clearly feeling no comfort from these explanations. When I first tried asking this question to a patient, I must have been inspired by Freud's theories about early traumatic experiences leaving a vulnerable emotional spot that can be brought to the surface by a similar experience later in life. It was gratifying to discover how effective this stratagem was and this led to further instances where I asked this question.

On another level, I believe this question can bring insight and relief in a much more effective manner than the ordinary, ritualistic transference interpretation of the patient's words and feelings. But, sadly, most present-day psychodynamic trainees are explicitly instructed never to ask questions to their patients.

Mariane

This was a senior architect who came to see me when she was in her early fifties. She was facing marital problems and we had several sessions when I saw her together with her husband. He was only two years older than her and they had been married for over twenty years. Both professed being happy in their marriage, but problems had arisen and their discussions had not resolved these issues, hence their coming to see me. They had stopped having sexual relations for quite a few years, but both claimed this was not the main reason for their conflicts.

One day, soon after they both made themselves comfortable, Mariane said she wanted to stop our meetings. She explained: "It is not that I feel we have solved our problems, but rather that I find these sessions far too difficult to cope with—I feel eviscerated" and after a pause: "We have important discussions here and there is something of visceral importance being talked about". After a pause, both Mariane and her husband told me of painful dreams they had had a couple of days earlier. Mr M had managed, without penetration, to get Mariane to reach orgasm, but as they fell asleep, both of them had dreams where they experienced pain, anxiety, fear, and wounds that bled profusely.

I found myself believing that the word "eviscerated" must have been chosen as a way of conveying painful, deeply significant feelings. Choosing my words carefully, I put it to them that I had the impression that they felt that vaginal penetration was damaging, something to be avoided—and the word "eviscerated" appeared to point to an experience of loss, of something being sucked out from inside the body. Mariane's husband burst out laughing, trying to retain his manners: "Oh! Come on! Those are cheap clichés!" Mariane was angry, she felt her husband might have offended me. Both of them were now silent.

And, watching my tone of voice, I asked her: "Have you ever lost a pregnancy?" She was shocked, frozen.

After considering how to proceed, Mariane told me that she was in her mid-forties when they went away on holiday and one evening as she was sure that menopause had set in, they had unprotected sex. But much to their surprise, she discovered a few weeks later she had become pregnant. Painful discussions followed and they agreed on a termination. Both of them were silent. Clearly, an old wound had unexpectedly been brought to the surface.

The following week the couple came to see me for a last meeting. I heard later from the mutual friends who had recommended they should see me that the marriage was "happy, steady as ever".

My interpretation of "evisceration", must have followed from my reaching the hypothesis that even if the penis had not sucked out the contents of the womb, its vaginal penetration had led to the eventual evisceration, the loss of a specific content of Mariane's body. The couple were shocked and surprised, but they made no explicit comment on my formulation. Both Mariane and her husband denied that this event had any significance in their subsequent sexual life.

I consider this case a good example of how attentive we must be to a patient's choice of words. It is obvious that any sentiment whatever can be formulated in no end of different ways, and this underlines the need to pay attention to the spoken words of the patient, and always consider the possibility that these words may be pointers to an unconscious thought seeking recognition.

Gloria

I was asked to see this seventeen-year-old girl because she was having trouble sleeping, suffering anxiety attacks and abdominal pains during the day and facing serious conflicts over what and when to eat. Gloria came to see me accompanied by both parents and, in reply to my question, said she did not mind they should stay in the room.

Mr and Mrs G had three children and Gloria was the youngest. While Gloria seemed to find it very difficult to engage in conversation with me, both her parents were keen to convey to me how worried they were about Gloria's symptoms. The two older children had never presented problems, but Gloria had complained of troubles all through her life. When only three years old she ended up having her appendix removed (subsequent microscopic investigation had shown that no pathology was present) and it was clear to me that this couple had always believed that Gloria's complaints were the surface manifestation of some undiagnosed disease.

I struggled to get a clear grasp of what pathology might be causing Gloria's personal experience of her situation. I decided to pick on the word "anorexia" that she had mentioned in passing—an aunt of hers suffered from a severe form of this. But Gloria told me that she knew the difference between "feeling fat" and "being fat", a statement that immediately convinced me that food was not the main source of her conflicts. We discussed her school and social life and Gloria was able to recount clashes and disagreements in a manner that suggested her being confident of her capacity to distinguish between a serious and a not-so-serious problem.

I was very aware of the fact that Mr G worked in the psychodynamic field and this made me choose my words when summing up my assessment of Gloria's problems. I said that I was sure that she had no psychiatric pathology and was simply facing ordinary, common adolescent developmental conflicts. I would recommend a few interviews with me, but I did not see this as particularly urgent.

We had a follow-up meeting two weeks later. A total turn around! Gloria had suffered no further discomforts and had raised no issues over what or when to eat. More importantly, she had gone to her music practice and managed to stay all day in school—all of which convinced her that her problems were over.

So, what was this "miracle" due to? I was smiling when I asked Gloria how could she explain this wonderful development? "Oh", she said, "it was your saying that this was a hiccup, not the beginning of any serious, long-term problem".

Mr G, who had come to this meeting, confirmed Gloria's words.

Six months later I had a letter from Mr G, expressing his gratitude. Gloria had achieved very good exam grades, she had now moved to a new school and was, quite simply, a very happy girl. "We could not have managed without you", he wrote.

Betty

This young lady was twenty-five years old when we had the interchange described below. I first met her many years earlier; she would come and see me for a few weeks and then stop when a particular problem was solved. When some new crisis occurred, she would contact me and attend sessions for a few weeks. She had a most captivating smile and a sharp intelligence. She had friends and colleagues, but her accounts of social outings would always contain an element of disappointment and sadness.

Her parents were divorced and Betty had never accepted any one of the men her mother moved closer to. She did keep in touch with her father, but this seemed quite a cold, distant link. Her relationship with her mother was fraught, and I heard no end of accounts where they ignored each other or clashed over minimal issues.

Betty came to see me one day and, taking into account the rather unusual degree of passion contained in her description of her parents' behaviour, I said: "Do you know? I think I am missing the point—what is at stake is not just your frustration about your parents not behaving in an honest manner, but rather your concern about *not saying* what you actually think of what they show you, of what you see—you know? Afraid of being open, perhaps losing control, not speaking as a well-behaved daughter, but voicing your feelings, you know? Being candid".

I noticed she had a funny smile on her face. She said: "do you know what book I was reading yesterday in the University library? *Candide*".

After a pause, still smiling, she told me which book she had been reading that day, before coming to her session: *The Plague*. I had to laugh: she did not need me to say that this is what she wished on her parents …

How can one explain this coincidence of thoughts? It brought to my mind the Portuguese saying "transmissão de pensamento" (we were on the same wavelength and knew of each other's thoughts). This episode was certainly surprising—and memorable.

"Clinging children"

One of the most significant discoveries I made over the years of my work with children and families concerns the so-called "clinging children". Whoever referred the family to me, they invariably quoted the mothers' expressions of anxiety and despair over their child's clinging behaviour and their conviction that there was something wrong with their child. Some mothers also managed to voice their irritation and resentment, as they felt invaded, restricted, dominated, and even abused by their child. Most referrers resorted to the common evaluation of the child behaving in a controlling and dominating manner. Seeing mother and child together in the consulting room, I was struck by a more complex picture. Given the opportunity, most mothers managed to express both their fears and also their exasperation. But focusing on the child's communications, what I detected was a sense of puzzlement, a fear of having something wrong in themselves and very often an intense dread of being abandoned by the mother. It is important to make explicit a feature implied in these cases: the fact that these mothers and children were referred to the Child Psychiatrist indicated that no organic, physical pathology had been found in these children—but the mothers had not been reassured by the professionals' repeated assertions that no pathology could be found in the children. I have described some of the cases showing these features in my book *The Language of Distress* (2016). What I kept finding were families where fathers tended to "not interfere", leaving the mother to care for the child—and considering the dyad mother-child, it was very difficult to decide who was "clinging". Or, to use different words: "who needs whom?"

And when I found myself thinking of this formulation, I was shocked to remember reaching the same conclusion when discussing the relationship between some spouses or partners, and, more surprising and disturbing, when considering the interaction between some seriously ill or incapacitated people and their carers. The world might have a clear idea of which spouse or which patient had a problem, but occasionally a closer observation led one to discover that the other spouse or the carer struggled with very complex feelings, one of which was the anxiety about the possibility that the patient or the unwell spouse would improve or, incredibly, die: they dreaded not only losing their sense of purpose, but also the painful confrontation with the complex multitude of feelings suddenly brought to the surface by the end of the shared predicament.

Suzanne

Suzanne was fifteen when referred to me. She had nightmares and during the day she was constantly contacting her mother, even though she found it difficult to explain why she had phoned, messaged, or reached out for her. Suzanne had a sister, who was three years older than her and then three younger siblings, the oldest of whom was seven years old.

Suzanne came to see me with her mother. Mrs S looked younger than her years, an attractive and intelligent urban planner who had stopped work just before giving birth to her younger children. Suzanne was a good-looking adolescent who quickly made herself at home in my consulting room, answering my questions and, occasionally exchanging comments with her mother.

Mrs S explained to me the family history. Some years before our meeting she and Mr S had decided to join an ultra-orthodox Jewish religious sect. I never forgot her summary of this transition: "I have kept the same husband—other than that, everything has changed!" I asked Suzanne what had brought her to see me. She was quite embarrassed when expressing her puzzlement about the frequency with which she tried to contact her mother. She also told me of her night-time problems: she struggled to fall asleep and then found herself disturbed by horrible dreams in which someone became ill or died. She looked at her mother and this was like opening a Pandora's box: they went on to give me an incredibly long list of people who had died since Suzanne's early childhood—and even though some of these were barely known to Suzanne, most of them were very close relatives or friends.

We were coming close to the time when I had to end our meeting. I was debating whether to urge Suzanne to have psychotherapy and whether I should also recommend similar help for Mrs S, since her account of the change in her life style had made me feel that she longed to resume her professional career, even though she was unable to make this move without professional help. But as I was thinking what to say, much to my surprise, Mrs S smiled, a warm, motherly loving expression on her face and told me that she thought she was overprotective. Whenever Suzanne is experiencing some problem, "My response", said Mrs S, "is to cuddle and comfort her". She then added, with a clear undertone of embarrassment: "in fact, I am lucky—Suzanne also tends to protect me".

At this point, the question came to the fore of my mind: who needs whom? Suzanne was moving into late adolescence and adulthood, but unconsciously (and perhaps quite consciously) she was aware of how much her mother counted on her closeness, her availability. How would she feel when choosing a University for further studies? I tried very hard to express my thought ("Congratulations! A happy pair!") using diplomatic words to underline the importance and possible consequences of this reassuring match of loving care.

Eventually, I told them that Suzanne would certainly benefit from psychotherapy and, indeed, she went to see a colleague of mine. I also offered to see Mrs S if she felt I could be of help. She thanked me and said she would keep this in mind and approach me if she needed help. I did not hear from Mrs S but some months later my colleague told me that Suzanne was a happier, less clinging adolescent.

Boris

This twenty-year-old young man had been referred to a psychotherapy organisation and I was asked to assess his suitability for therapy under a trainee. We only had one meeting but this brought out an unexpected finding that I thought justified this description. In our interview we covered many areas of Boris' life and when I decided to give him a trial interpretation, it resulted in a reaction that left me wondering about one's capacity to find that crucial significant datum among all the subjects being discussed.

Boris was very tall and presented a modest but elegant figure. He was very tense and found it difficult to articulate his words. As a child he was considered small for his age and was bullied at school. Academically very successful, he made good progress, but very unexpectedly he had a breakdown during his university studies. After recovery, he decided to interrupt his studies and became engaged in various jobs, which required living with his parents. This proved an intolerable choice and he soon moved out.

Boris applied for therapy because of his permanent state of tension and depression, sometimes finding himself crying with no clear explanation for such a development. Teachers, employers, friends, and colleagues all admired his intelligence and urged him to write and publish papers and to become a teacher—no use, his self-esteem was far too poor and he had ground to a halt, totally unable to produce any work. He did have a good circle of friends and over the years had formed long-term relationships with several young women but now he tried to keep himself away from everyone.

Discussing his early years and his family relationships, he told me of close relationships with two sisters (one older, the other younger than him) and of instances where his mother was warm and affectionate to him. Boris played the piano and he told me of his father's love of music that had led him to have a huge collection of records that he would play whenever resting at home. But the parents had a very fraught relationship and Boris told me of how vivid were his memories of sitting alone with his mother, who was trying to comfort him. Music, however, linked Boris to his father's world and it was with a shaky voice that Boris told me that the one and only example he had of his father's referring to his piano playing was the harsh question "have you done your practice?"

Both his sisters were still single and I formed the idea that all three siblings had developed a very painful, traumatic image of what marriage and child bearing meant in life. As Boris told me of his depression and the medication prescribed for his emotional state, I kept being impressed by the contrast between his self-image and the repeated words of praise and admiration that had proved so ineffectual.

Eventually, I decided to check on Boris' response to interpretations of his unconscious feelings (an important datum when long-term insight therapy is being considered). I put it to him that however much tutors and bosses and friends praised him, this was of no help—apparently, only being recognised by his father would make a difference. And Boris burst out crying. He said he had not cried for months, though he often struggled with tears when not taking anti-depressive medication.

Seeing his reaction, I apologised for my comment and Boris said it was unfair for me to do it when this seemed to be the only time we would meet—but added that it was a valued realisation and that he would now be able to think further about its implications.

I thought Boris would find help in regular psychotherapy and recommended he should be offered a vacancy. Unfortunately, I had no information about further developments.

Gertrude

This young woman in her late twenties applied for a psychotherapy vacancy and I saw her for an assessment. It soon became clear that her motivation and her emotional structure made her an ideal training case. Intelligent, articulate, insightful—she needed help to make sense of her life experiences: these were simply too difficult to accept as part of ordinary family life.

Gertrude's application form recounted some of her past history and present life. A very successful academic and leading an active social life, I was sure that not a single person in her environment would ever guess what Gertrude had gone through in her life. Our meeting is presented here because it depicts so convincingly the power of the unconscious and the meaning of dreams.

Gertrude's mother committed suicide when she was four years old, but this was a taboo subject. Her father had suffered a motorcycle accident in his youth and this left him with a severe incapacity in his lower limbs. He married another woman with whom Gertrude had a close relationship: this lady had a child from a previous marriage and went on to have another child with Gertrude's father. When Gertrude was in her early teens the older one of her step-brothers committed suicide and the couple split up soon afterwards. I was surprised to learn that her father went on to become the third husband of another woman who happened to have lost her parents in very tragic circumstances. Too much! And I could not stop myself from saying that considering so many traumatic events, one might think they came from a fictional account.

Gertrude had tears in her eyes for most of these accounts and when I made my comment she did manage to smile; it was obvious that she had often wondered about what fate had brought to her. But now she told me that the previous night she had had a dream. "I don't believe in dreams and I tend to ignore them … but I dreamt that I had met a Scandinavian young man and fallen in love with him. Indeed this was an attractive fellow I have met recently—and his name is (she spelt it) L e i f—and, guess what? In his language this is pronounced *life*!"

Surely, considering Gertrude's traumatic experiences of loss, no doubt can be left about Freud's theory about dreams representing wish-fulfilments?

Anne

Since health insurance companies demand a medical assessment of a patient before he/she can have private psychotherapy with a lay professional, I was asked to see this young woman in her mid-thirties. Exceptionally intelligent and attractive, I was shocked to learn of the problems she had faced in her life. She held a senior position in a bank, but she had gone through quite a series of other jobs.

Anne found out quite early in life that she could not read, but incredibly learnt to memorise texts. Apparently she was never referred to a psychological assessment and throughout life she learnt of stratagems to avoid having to write any texts. Anne moved through many schools and eventually decided to stop. Home life was quite catastrophic.

She said that her father treated her mother and her siblings (two brothers) as slaves and he had a particular obsession over Anne's weight. He sent her to health farms as soon as she put on a few kilograms—and she pronounced a precious sentence: "he was never interested in me—only in how I looked".

Considering her background perhaps it was not surprising that she had seen "loads of therapists", but contrary to most people in this situation, she added: "the trouble is my poor staying power …" Weight had been the main motive leading her to seek therapy, but now she wanted relief of her depressive feelings. She had even thought of cutting her wrists, but "I wouldn't do it—too much of a coward …"

Anne was married when she came to see me, but the couple were struggling with serious problems. She described her husband as the kindest, most considerate, intelligent, and warm man she had ever met—and they had had a very active sexual life that Anne described as most enjoyable. However, from the day they decided to get married—sex stopped. Plenty of problems to discuss in therapy! But it was her weight that most worried and troubled her, making her seek therapy. "That is one of the reasons why I do not want to have children: I don't want to put on weight". She must have noticed my expression of surprise (she had not impressed me as particularly overweight), because she went on to say: "I know it is not rational, but there you are: I still feel just as fat as I've ever been …"

Even if Anne had "warned" me about her "poor staying power", I did write my medical report stating that she did not suffer from any serious psychiatric illness and urged the health insurers to support her long-term therapy. I could only hope that her new therapist would succeed in developing a relationship that would enable Anne to stay in therapy as long as necessary. I can only apologise for the fact that I did not have any follow-up information from Anne or from my colleague who went on to treat her.

Fanny

Fanny's best friend organised a party to celebrate Fanny's birthday. When she got there, Fanny found that her friend had invited many friends of her own, but only two of Fanny's friends. She became intensely upset and her mother urged her to see me. Fanny came to see me on her own. She was an attractive eighteen-year-old who made herself easily at home and was happy to answer my questions and clarify any misunderstandings. As Fanny told me of her resentment and the resultant feelings of panic, I was surprised (amused?) to hear her informing me that she had discovered that a horoscope stated that that particular week of her birthday would bring frustrating, painful experiences.

Fanny's father was a successful businessman, but spent most of his time travelling abroad. Her mother worked as a secretary and two older brothers were at University. Fanny felt she had always been "everybody's" favourite, loved and praised by family, teachers, and friends, and yet she claimed to have a powerful feeling of failure—she had dreamt of becoming a famous artist and yet …

Fanny had attended several schools, repeatedly complaining of feeling unhappy and wanting to move on to another one. When I saw her, Fanny was going through her GCSE exams; she obtained an A* in Art, getting B, C, and E in other subjects. She had a wide circle of friends, but "none of them long-term". Speaking of these relationships, I was surprised to hear her saying that "if I want to cheat, fool anyone, I can easily do it", and I thought this was a sentiment linked to the broken off relationships with friends and colleagues.

Fanny's closest relative was her paternal grandmother and she told me that they spoke every day, sometimes for over an hour. Great-grandmother and the maternal grandmother were described as "monsters". Fanny had reasonably close relations with aunts and uncles, and she made a point of telling me that many of those had been seeing analysts for endless years—something she definitely did not want to copy.

I next saw Fanny together with her mother. This lady spoke in a very agitated manner, going into minor details of every subject she took up. She was obviously worried about her daughter and a most significant exchange was Mrs F saying her daughter was "very nervous and unhappy" and Fanny replying "You don't really know me …" to which Mrs F said "I do, I know you much better than you think!"

We decided I would see Fanny for some sessions in order to get a clearer idea of her needs. After a few meetings, I was going on holidays for two weeks, but on the date of our last appointment, Mrs F phoned me to say that Fanny was ill: her close friend, Bob, had let her down and Fanny had "gone to pieces", she lay in bed, crying and refusing to eat or do anything. When I returned to London and resumed work, Fanny did not come at our arranged time. I phoned them and found Mrs F in total panic: Fanny had lost ten kilograms, refused to leave home, said she did not want to live even though she denied wanting to kill herself. We arranged another time for me to see Fanny. She was clearly obsessed with Bob. She gave me the count of let downs: he had let her down three times and she had let him down five times. And it turned out that they had not seen each other for three months!

Fanny described Bob as unreliable and insecure, but "I love him!" And she claimed that Bob also loved her and enjoyed spending time together. And several further sessions were focused on events between the two of them. I had the impression that these two youngsters had got stuck in a tantalising, tormenting relationship and, sadly, my interpretations that they had become a unit, the two sides of the same coin, projecting on each other features of their personal experiences, did not produce any change.

And then came peace, but this did not last long. One session, a couple of months later, brought forward a Fanny I had not seen before. She was due to take a test at college and, if she passed, Fanny said her father would buy her a Jeep. She went on to explain to me that she had chosen this reward because she hates trains and buses, she hates "stupid crowds", "they are dirty, messy, undeserving, envious". I could not hide my surprise: I had never suspected any such views! Fanny decided to itemise her list of contemptible creatures: poor people, handicapped ones, gays, sick, small babies, people over seventy/eighty ("they should be allowed to die: they cannot live on their own, need help all the time!"). "Babies are messy, demanding, creepy—of course I will never have one!" As if all this did not cover her prejudices, she added: "oh, yes! If I ever have a child, I will never allow him to be gay!" Much along this line, she remembered going to a club to see a film with her father and discovering that this was a gay club: she clung to her father and when she got home she "had four or five showers: I was *so* disgusted!"

Somehow, I found myself asking her if she knew what "eugenics" meant. She did: "that was what Hitler did, no? But, no, I don't want to kill anyone, but certainly if all these people disappeared, the world would be a happier place." I suppose this sentiment should be considered together with another of Fanny's image of herself in the world: "as soon as I love or like someone, they turn against me and leave me".

Fanny did not obtain good grades in her exams, which threatened to spoil her plan of going to a University abroad. Her remedy shocked and scared me: she went to speak to the director and showed him her tablet where she had recorded teachers speaking badly of students and of other teachers. She informed him that her uncle was a journalist and she would give him this material to be published—and it worked: her grades were changed to A, A, and B.

This was one of my worst failures. When first assessing Fanny I did worry about some underlying serious pathology, but her relationship with Bob must have clouded my scrutiny, so that when these viral prejudices and psychopathic behaviour came up, I was lost. Our meetings were never regular, with Fanny cancelling many sessions. Eventually, Fanny went abroad for visits and she felt that she "had enough" of our work. I certainly had not managed to give her any significant help.

Vera

This Dutch young woman in her late twenties had applied for a psychotherapy vacancy and I interviewed her to assess her suitability for being seen by a trainee. I have no follow-up to report, but I thought of describing our meeting because it shows the importance of finding the right questions to ask in the course of a consultation.

Reading Vera's application form I had been impressed by the emphasis she had given to multiple suicide attempts. When she was about eight years old, she remembers keeping a sharp, pointed, kitchen knife in her bedside drawer "for about a year". She often put it to her chest and thought that *if* she pushed it in, she would die. Somehow, her parents never found the knife: "they allowed us, children, a lot of privacy". She said that she still has a scar over the point where the knife touched her skin, but she denied that the wound ever bled to any significant extent. Later, she would attempt suicide mostly when drunk. The latest attempt occurred after her boyfriend left her apartment ("I let him go"—"oh, I can be quite demanding: if I wanted him to stay, I would scream and shout and get him to stay!"). She found herself continuing to drink and eventually she was outside her fourth-floor window, threatening to jump. The people on the road called an ambulance and she was taken to a hospital. She decided to stop drinking since then.

I asked Vera to tell me, in Dutch, what thoughts she had when, as a child, she thought about death. "This is not fair! I've never wanted to be here!" (She translated it for me) This puzzled me, since I wondered how she had come to formulate this particular existential quandary. Vera explained that her father was a zoologist and that he had, from early on, told her about biological subjects. She remembers speaking at school about things that other children could not understand. She recalls thinking that if, instead of that particular sperm of her father's having fecundated her mother, it had been a different one, then she would not have been born.

She had mentioned in her application form her "absent libido", even though she had managed to have a happy relationship with her boyfriend for over two years. When Vera was telling me about her parents' life, she described a rather unhappy picture. Some comment of hers gave me the impression that they had not been born in Holland. Considering Vera's present move away from home, I indicated my interest and asked for details. Father had been born in Holland, but his father was Swedish. Mother had a Polish mother, a communist who had fled to Holland at the time of the Second World War and a New Zealander father who was studying in Holland. And here came my second fundamental question: was the maternal grandmother Jewish? Yes, she was Jewish and Vera was very aware of her Jewish background, having studied the Holocaust very seriously. The maternal grandmother had gone through dramatic and painful steps before settling in Holland with the man she had married. In other words, Vera had known from very early on what it meant to live under constant danger of being killed—and the struggles faced by those who managed to survive.

I thought that Vera had unconsciously identified with her maternal grandmother and came to see herself as exposed to similar threats and then experiencing life as signifying a continuous exposure to the danger of death. I was convinced that these painful events in Vera's life must have led her to wonder why/how had she been "chosen" to struggle through them and, consequently, caused her to be so aware of the fragility of being alive—when death can be seen as a step that puts an end to the pain of living.

Ivan

This thirty-year-old gentleman was an interesting diagnostic problem. His complaints led to a diagnosis of hyper-excited personality, but beyond the general features of his presentation, he suffered from anxieties of a phobic nature that presumably resulted from experiences he had had through his life. The problem? If and when these phobic anxieties were relieved, would that make any difference to his sense of self?

Ivan had grown up in a rural province in the East. He came to work in the UK, but he would often return to his place of origin to visit his family, to whom he was very attached. He had a couple of girlfriends and reported happy relationships, but he was determined not to have children and this had led to these relationships coming to an end. He worked in the building industry and had no trouble in finding jobs. He decided to consult me after a colleague was impressed by Ivan's continuous agitation and convinced him to "give it a try" and see me.

Ivan told me how he was "forever scared, anticipating disasters". Noises, flashes of light, "anything" could set off his sense of dread. Sleeping was an ordeal. When he was ten years old, his mother had taken him to a doctor who gave him drugs that he took for several years. He was very attached to his paternal grandmother, with whom he lived most of the time. He was very upset when she died from a severe stroke three years before his coming to see me.

Ivan's father was epileptic and before the fits he would always give a huge scream—and Ivan remembered going to his parents' bedroom and finding his mother trying to hold his father down and comfort him. Ivan mentioned very briefly names and ages of four siblings, with whom he did not have close involvement. Ivan struggled with a problem that I would never be able to guess: he had an obsession with knives. He had never attacked anybody, but he still *hid* every single knife in his house "in case (he) might lose control" and kill his companion or any visitor.

The reference to knives as killing instruments, led me to ask whether he followed or knew about Halal or Kosher—he did not know these words and I explained these Muslim and Jewish ways of killing animals since they were not allowed to eat animal flesh containing blood. This explanation made him jump—he suddenly remembered his father killing pigs in their farm: and the fact that the animals would always utter a terrible scream. It was hardly necessary for me to call his attention to the link he had made between the pigs' scream and that of his father's when having an epileptic fit.

I urged Ivan to have further sessions, but his style of life made this virtually unrealistic. I also suggested he asked his GP for medication that might relieve his sense of anxiety. He did contact me a couple of weeks after our consultation and said that his obsession with knives had abated—and thanked me for this.

This case is another example of finding a question that turns a passing remark into the door to a crucial feature of the patient's experiences.

Much as Vera, Ivan was also obsessed by knives—but these appeared to contain different unconscious meanings to each of them.

Terry

This is an example of those cases where analysis may lead the patient to understand the unconscious reasons for his problems, but still not to obtain a change. Sadly, this is exactly what is depicted in the classical joke of those who deride psychoanalysis: two friends meet and one asks the other: "you used to wet the bed and you went to an analyst: did it help?" The reply: "well … I still wet the bed, but now I know why I do it …"

Terry was forty years old when he was referred to me. He was a good-looking, intelligent man but he was not satisfied with his position in life. He had struggled to achieve a steady, successful, professional position but he was not happy with it. He had been through a number of relationships, which sooner or later came to an end. Not surprisingly, he often found himself depressed—and the medication prescribed by his GP did not produce the desired effects.

Terry was the youngest of three children, all born just over one year apart. When he was eight years old, his father left home and it was only many years later that one of his siblings met their father in a supermarket. Their mother forbade them from bringing the father home and, unfortunately, soon afterwards they had to take father into hospital. He had had internal bleeding from a cancer metastasis and died days later.

Terry spent his mid and late adolescence travelling round the world and eventually decided to join a University. Here he met a woman and moved into her house. He smiled when telling me that he suffered from "excess testosterone". However, with this lady, much as went on to happen with several further relationships, after a time "it all dies" and he loses interest in sex. And something similar happened with the jobs Terry found for himself: always successful and valued, but losing interest and moving on after a time.

Terry claimed he wanted "to improve myself, to be happier with myself". He once had hypnotherapy to stop smoking and it worked, but this had not produced any other helpful effects. His sister had managed to get married and have children, but his brother had only just managed to get married. When he came to see me, Terry had been working in the same establishment for eight years and he had also been living together with a woman for four years. As in earlier relationships, their sexual life was virtually non-existent. But Terry added that they managed to talk about it and "she accepts that our closeness makes up for it". I was surprised when he quoted words from a psychologist he admired: "Peck wrote that falling in love is to break the boundaries of the self and to merge entities." I thought this was very significant and urged him to elaborate on it. He soon came to express that "*what I resent and fear is their dependence on me*".

I was convinced that we had reached a central, basic point. I thought Terry's unconscious was "not allowing" him to articulate the crucial words and I tried to get him to draw, but he refused this. I went on to write down his words, trying to probe his past experiences, hoping this would help us find "the turning point". After a while, Terry remembered a lady-friend who he "really felt she could pull me down the precipice". And what was so different in that relationship? "She became obsessed with having a child …"

Terry could recognise his "conviction", his dread that having a child brought about the destruction of the "self", the independent, self-sufficient "I". Apparently, a couple could stay together, loving each other, understanding and accepting each other's needs—but the arrival of a child signified the end of this harmonious engagement. I saw Terry for quite a few months, and at the time when he decided to stop his sessions, he still enjoyed his relationship with his partner—but no question of having a child.

Rachel

This young lady applied for a vacancy at a psychotherapy training organisation and I saw her for an assessment. This means that, unfortunately, I do not have information about developments, but I am describing the case because it is one more example of how "survivors" find it difficult to fulfil their potentials.

Rachel was thirty years old when I met her. An intelligent and attractive young woman, she felt unhappy about her relationships and her professional progress. She had a complex family history. Maternal grandmother was depressed and was treated with electroconvulsive therapy (ECT) and many drugs. Grandfather was a builder and Rachel felt he was mostly responsible for bringing up their children.

But Rachel's mother was also a needy, fragile person and Rachel had spent long periods at the grandparents' home. This involved even longer periods after her younger sister was diagnosed as suffering from cerebral palsy.

Rachel's mother worked at a charity, but she was frequently drunk and I was left with the impression that Rachel had become the "caretaker" of mother and sister. Both father and mother had always treated Rachel as their confidante and she was well aware of how this made her self-conscious in her approach to life and people. And perhaps the main reason for my account here was Rachel having been told that her sister's birth resulted from mother "being raped" by her father—and also that her mother had been very keen to terminate the pregnancy from which she (Rachel) was born!

Rachel experienced "panic attacks": intense anxiety and an urge "to seek shelter". She told me how she "can even feel paranoid, but luckily I manage to tell myself that I'm thinking nonsense". Rachel started her first relationship when she was twenty. This lasted only a few months and she then had a boyfriend for nearly three years—and near the end of this affair she became pregnant. She had no doubt about her wish to have a termination, but having to see a counsellor, she became very upset when realising this was nearly the same age when her mother had given birth to her. But she still had a termination. She did not have a boyfriend at the time of our meeting.

Rachel had obtained University degrees in quite unusual subjects and I had a strong impression that she had not managed to find a position where her potentials would be turned into reality. She was concentrating on helping, caring, tendering to the needs of young people, but always in very menial positions. I could only hope that therapy would help her to find her way to a harmonious and fulfilling relationship, as well as professional positions where she might fulfil her potential abilities.

Rita

This young lady was in her late twenties when she applied for a vacancy in a psychotherapy society. I came to the end of our consultation feeling guilty—she needed and deserved help, but I felt she needed to be seen by a therapist with more clinical experience than a student in training. I managed to find another establishment that offered Rita a vacancy for her therapy. However I do not have any follow-up information about Rita's progress.

Rita had spent most of her life struggling with difficult and painful feelings. She was happy to tell me about her family and her personal development: intelligent and articulate, this was not a problem. But however aware of her emotional struggles, Rita had not succeeded in overcoming a recurrent conflict: "I do not feel suicidal, but I definitely have no desire to live". When she was sixteen years old she "walked in front of a bus"—she was not hit and had no clear memories of events preceding or following the event. At one point, she joined a club of cyclists who planned to ride from London to Scotland—practising for this venture she was hit by a car and fractured her shoulder. Rita summed up these feelings saying that she was "all the time fighting an impulse to lie in bed and stay there ..."

Rita had had a couple of intimate relationships, but these had broken down for various reasons. Her application for therapy was clearly one more example of her recurrent impulse to achieve change and fulfil her potentials, rather than giving in to her self-destructive feelings. Rita had an older brother who had "done all the right things", qualifying from University, getting married, having children, keeping up a good career. He had always tried to support Rita and her eyes filled with tears when expressing her gratitude to him. But ... but ... it turned out that from earliest childhood Rita felt she was "all the time" involved with her mother in verbal and physical fights of increasing severity. Many years later her mother told Rita that she reminded her of "her earlier self". Rita's words were "we are very intertwined": an accurate assessment.

At the time of our meeting, Rita was involved with a man several years younger than her—she said he was "sweet, kind, protective". Earlier, she had been involved for four years with a man who drank too much.

I was intensely aware of the need to "hit the iron while it is hot", that is, not to delay the provision of a therapy vacancy, but I felt Rita had to be treated by an experienced professional, not a student. I decided to describe her story here because the "suicidal patient" is one of the most difficult challenges in the psychotherapy consulting room and Rita's story is a typical example of the virtual impossibility of establishing a clear prognosis of the chances of psychotherapy succeeding to reach and develop that person's right/desire to live.

Jessica

This lady was in her late thirties when she consulted me. She had seen the counsellor at her GP's practice for the six sessions allowed by the

NHS. Jessica sought help because she suffered panic attacks after the break-up of her marriage. Having found these sessions very helpful, she came to see me to discuss the possibility of having regular long-term psychotherapy. She had little regular income and I put her in touch with the organisations that might offer her a vacancy she could afford.

Jessica's parents were born in different Caucasian countries and after their marriage lived in both of these, as well as in other Middle-Eastern countries. Her father was mostly a non-participating figure in the family life, while her mother was "forever shouting and shrieking". Apparently, when Jessica reached late adolescence, she and her older brother plucked up the courage to challenge their mother "and she stopped her screams".

In her early twenties Jessica moved to Scandinavia where she formed a close relationship with a boyfriend, but as in previous similar relationships, they had no sex. I was surprised to learn that Jessica only managed to have actual intercourse with people she happened to meet at parties or other similar "one off" situations. After a few years, Jessica moved to London and not long afterwards started a relationship with a man she came to marry five years before I saw her. She described him as a compulsive drinker and smoker, who seldom agreed to have sex. Perhaps predictably the day came when, seeing him arriving home with a bottle of whisky, Jessica flipped and started a colossal row. He left the house and after a half an hour she went outside and found him sitting on a park bench. The argument started again and, much to her horror, Jessica hit him across the face. He had never hit her and Jessica was so stunned that she told him they should really part ways.

Then came the moment I would never have guessed was possible. Considering Jessica's reaction to her own behaviour, I asked her if this loss of control had ever happened before in her life. Her face froze, tears came to her eyes and she said, struggling to find the words: "I just remembered one day hitting my dog—can you imagine this? How could I? He was my child!"

Jessica certainly needed help to fulfil her potentials in professional terms and also in choosing a partner with whom she might feel able to form a family. Unfortunately, I had no further news from her.

Bianca

This girl was nine years old when her parents were urged to consult me about her problems. She had already been seen by a large number of professionals in other countries and most of them agreed on a diagnosis of ADHD. She was prescribed Ritalin, but her reaction to this drug varied because of unknown factors, so she was on no medication most of the time. The parents came to see me a few times, but Bianca herself never agreed to see me.

From the parents' account it was quite difficult to reach a clear picture of Bianca's problems. Both parents were born in Holland, but had come to live in England when Bianca was only three years old. Senior architects, they had a busy life, but had always kept in close touch with their families of origin. Mrs B was in her mid-thirties when she came to see me and Mr B was a few years older than her. They told me that Bianca had a long history of fears, panic attacks, school problems, and severe sleeping difficulties. Quoting these symptoms, Mrs B would not fail to mention how they interfered with the family life. A recent example she gave me was their having to cancel flight tickets they had purchased to visit the family in Holland—because Bianca complained of severe dizziness.

I asked the couple to give me a description of their backgrounds. Sadly, the mothers of both of them had suffered from cancer and Mr B's mother had died rather recently from a heart attack. But the main point that emerged was that they had been on the brink of separating several times because most of the time they spent together they would engage in shouting matches. To my surprise and disbelief, they were convinced that Bianca and her younger sister had no knowledge of their marital problems.

Mr and Mrs B showed me psychologists' reports on Bianca. These mentioned how she would often not manage to understand things she read, clumsiness when organising things, difficulty in concentrating on tasks—but time and again they emphasised her brightness. Considering the data I was struck by a neurologist's report stating that he had found that Bianca's visual neural pathways were discordant in the two eyes. I told Mr and Mrs B that my impression was that it was most unlikely that Bianca suffered from ADHD—instead, I thought she had a learning difficulty (Dyslexia? Dyspraxia?) and her general behaviour suggested anxiety about loss—a school friend of hers had just lost his father, she had lost her paternal grandmother, and I would suspect she might also be scared of her parents divorcing. Surprisingly, Mrs B confirmed my words, saying that Bianca had asked her many times whether she would divorce her father—this coming in spite of her earlier assertion that the children did not know of their quarrels.

I went on to voice my opinion that their images of Bianca were dramatically different. Mr B smiled and said he tended to be firm with Bianca, but his wife was more indulgent. He quoted what happens when Bianca needs to have a bath: he insists she must do it and she complains of his loud demands. Contrary to this, Mrs B will plead with her to have the bath. I gave them my interpretation of these accounts. I said that, to my mind, Bianca would take her father's attitude as a vote of confidence, a certainty that she was able to have a bath. Contrariwise, it was likely that Bianca might take her mother's pleas as demonstrating a wish to protect her, that is, she is a weak child and needs help. Both of them were shaken by my words. After a pause, Mrs B managed to express her feelings: "She is like glued to my neck and sucks my blood away!" Being careful with my words and tone of voice, I said, almost apologetically, that it was possible that Bianca was feeling that her mother needed her company. But I would never guess Mrs B's reply: she was shocked, her voice trembled and she said she had just remembered that when she was a child, she refused to sleep anywhere away from home, because she believed that her mother needed her company.

Mr and Mrs B now went on to recount memories of Bianca's early years; examples of her cleverness and dexterity, as well as situations requiring help. The atmosphere in the room had changed quite dramatically. I have been describing the progress of two meetings and when I met the Bs again, we continued this analysis of Bianca's personality and it was quite noticeable that Mrs B did not see her daughter as so fragile and needy/demanding as when we had first met. New developments were taking place, since Bianca was placed in a new school that had the reputation of paying much closer attention to the needs of individual children.

A few months later, the headmaster of this school sent me a report where he had written: "There have not been any suggestions from our staff that she may have ADHD. She needed a little help to adjust to a new class and I enjoy her bouncy, outgoing personality." Some more weeks went by and Bianca's teacher sent me a message: "Bianca has made good progress in all subjects and shown a great deal of enthusiasm for her learning. She has grown in confidence and produced good results. I feel Bianca is a student who needed to increase her self-esteem in order to access the curriculum. She is now self-motivated and willing to approach activities with a positive attitude. She is a pleasure to teach".

I found this is a very moving example of the influence a mother's attitude can have on a child's development. I do believe that Mrs B's insight into the origins and the consequences of her "protecting" Bianca and the resultant "stepping back" was the key to this girl's progress.

Oscar

I am sure there must be some brain structure that leads most, if not all, of our thinking along the lines of causality. One can see this in operation in any ordinary conversation. One person recounts an event and mentions an accompanying feeling—and immediately the other person will put forward an explanation for the experience of that particular feeling. Right? Wrong? However plausible the causal explanation, it remains impossible to guess whether it will make sense, let alone affect that first person's experience. The usual cliché is something like "oh, well … could be … but I'm not really sure that I feel anything like that …"

This dynamic is what struck me very forcibly when I saw Oscar, a pharmacist in his mid-fifties. At the recommendation of a friend he came to see me and, as he sat down, he explained the reason for his visit: "You cured my friend of his worries and I hope you will also cure me!" This was said in a humorous, friendly tone of voice. After a sociable exchange, I asked Oscar to give me an idea of his problems and of his background. He had been born in Scotland, where his father ran a bakery with his mother's help. Many years before his birth, his parents had had another son who died from a cerebral tumour when eight years old. "My mother always said I was a mistake … well, she did mean well, she wanted me to value that she had brought me to life …"

Oscar had a successful academic career, obtaining a scholarship for his university studies and later achieving progress to become an assistant lecturer. He married Maryanne in his late twenties and after four years she gave birth to twins, but one of them died soon after birth. She blamed herself for this, since labour pains had started just after they had had sex. From that point the couple's sexual life changed and Oscar said he had accepted that it was Maryanne who now decided if and when to have sex. But after a few years she wanted to have another child and sex became more frequent again—virtually disappearing from the marriage after this child was born. Telling me these facts, Oscar was quite vehement in stating that he had no feelings about his dead child—or about the death of his brother. It was indeed puzzling to hear him say "no feelings about it ..." when he had also told me of being taken every year by his aunt to visit the grave of his dead brother. I asked whether Maryanne or his sons knew and had particular feelings about these losses—and Oscar replied that he had no idea, he had never asked them, nor had the subject ever been raised in the family's conversations.

Oscar complained about his insomnia: for many years he struggled to fall asleep, but would then wake up after two hours and wander around, not succeeding in falling asleep again. Over the years various doctors had put forward different diagnoses and he had been put on various drugs, but with no success. His general social personality was also affected: "all my friends know that when I'm annoyed or frustrated I just go icy and become quiet and sarcastic ... I'm terrified of making mistakes ... I'm quite strict, demanding of my performance in life ..."

Considering our discussion, I put it to Oscar that my impression was that "death" was an ever present threat that took on various guises in different circumstances—with his constant worry about making mistakes that might bring about serious, dangerous, and unpredictable consequences. He made some grimaces, as if able to understand my reasoning, but his comment was to state quite firmly that he had no such feelings at all. I decided to add that whenever anything did go wrong, just as his wife, he blamed himself—but a fundamental difference existed: he thought he was rational, but Maryanne was irrational. I was rewarded with a warm smile for this comment.

A new appointment? Oscar said he wanted to think about it, but he sent me a message a week later, stating that, for the moment, he wanted to let matters rest.

Leonard

In their paper on "Replacement Children", Cain and Cain (1964) reported from their work:

> For example, the continual "clogged" throat, gasping for air, and preoccupation with things being caught in his throat of the boy whose brother choked on a piece of bread; and "arm pains" of the girl whose brother died of leukemia and had experienced peculiar sensations in his arms. (Cain & Cain, 1964, p. 450)

In line with these cases, I would like to describe my consultation with a boy aged ten whose brother (Phillip) had died of cancer five years earlier. Leonard was presenting behavioural problems at home and at school and by the time I saw him, he had already been seen by other professionals and given various diagnoses, mainly ADHD. When the parents brought him to see me, they also brought his sister, aged twelve. Parents were architects and they decided to see "still another professional" because they were urged to do it by a friend of theirs who was also a colleague/friend of mine. At her suggestion, the parents wrote to me, describing Leonard's problems and giving me a summary picture of the family, in which they mentioned Phillip's death.

Telling me about his life, Leonard mentioned that when he was six years old he had suffered a fall from a slide that caused a hairline fracture to his arm bone. After we went through my usual preliminaries of the consultation, I asked the boy to make a drawing of his family and, to everybody's surprise, the girl also asked for some paper to make the same drawings. As they finished, I looked at the pictures and, making no comment, asked the parents to look at them. Both of them were shocked and, virtually in unison, said "but neither of you drew Phillip!" Leonard apologetically mentioned that he had no image of Phillip and the parents reminded him of how many photos they have of him throughout their house. The children were clearly embarrassed and, timidly and determinedly, went back to the pages of paper and made new drawings of the family, but now including an image of Phillip.

Their brother had died of bone cancer and Leonard had drawn both of Phillip's forearms forming a distorted angle with the arms. Being careful with my voice, I called his attention to the fact that he had drawn his own upper limbs with a similar distortion to what he had depicted in Phillip's image. He was surprised, but made no comment, though his facial expression suggested he had grasped the implication of the way he had depicted his arms. Mr L was fascinated by this unexpected configuration, but Mrs L concentrated on asking me for guidance as to how she could help Leonard to improve his behaviour. I explained that the more she would try "to help", the higher the possibility of Leonard believing there was "something wrong in him that called for special help". I had the impression that Mr L could see the logic of my argument, but not his wife.

Because the family lived very far from my consulting room, they said they would prefer to wait before making another appointment. I urged them to find a psychotherapist who could see Leonard. The boy was visibly disappointed by his parents' reaction to my words. In fact, he had told them that he would like to see me again. They asked why and he answered: "because I learnt a lot today"—a wonderful compliment! I gave him my email address and said he should feel free to contact me.

Since I did not hear from the family over the following week, I decided to write a note to Leonard, in which I called his attention to the important difference between *feeling* and *knowing*. I could only send it to his parents' email address and hope that they would show it to him.

The family never contacted me again.

Freddy

This is another example of a child presenting symptoms that lead to repeated referrals, tests, and prescriptions—where taking into account the details of that child's life, it becomes difficult to establish the extent to which the complaints stem from the child's psychological endowment or, instead, result from the environment in which the child lives.

Freddy was ten years old when his GP referred him to me: sleeping problems, unusual/puzzling attitudes and difficulties in relationships that the parents were unable to help him with. I found him a friendly, intelligent boy who quickly made himself at home, quite happy to answer my questions and describe his anxieties. The GP had been consulted because Freddy kept referring to a film he had watched with his father, in which a man was killed in a particularly sadistic manner.

The parents had brought Freddy to the interview and allowed him to answer my questions without commenting or correcting his words. We spoke about Freddy's life at home and at school and eventually he told me about his life terrors. It was monsters that he kept thinking about—and, pointing to his father, he said: "it's *his* fault!" and I was told of how Mr F will, every evening, watch horror movies on TV. The parents said they no longer allowed Freddy to sit with his father to watch these films …

When I commented that Freddy felt his life in danger and, therefore, he was afraid that he might die, he corrected me: "*It's not death I'm frightened of, but of dying!*" I was really struck by this sentence! We met again two weeks later. Eventually, we came to focus on Freddy's nighttime behaviour: he will get out of his bed and walk along the corridor and, often, go to his parents' bedroom. He explained this was how he dealt with the frightening ideas that tormented him as soon as he lay down on his bed. I reminded him of his poignant, concise statement about death, he elaborated on it: "If you had to die from a bullet on the head or having each finger pulled out, then each toe pulled out and then bit by bit, each bit of your body—which would you choose?" And now Mrs F said "he asks this question very often, you know". Considering Freddy's descriptions of his fears, I decided to give him my interpretation: "You said it is not the dream that wakes you up? I think that you wake up and then you don't know whether you are really alive or not—and this is why you go searching to see if others are still alive and to make sure that you are also alive". Surprisingly, he nodded, "I think that's it …" and repeated my words!

I saw Freddy and Mrs F again one month later. The level of tension between them seemed to have abated. They had agreed that Freddy should read in bed until falling asleep. Mrs F had also promised him rewards for sleeping the whole night without leaving his room. And then Freddy put forward an interesting suggestion: "Perhaps you will close the door of my room when I go to bed?" and, to my total astonishment, Mrs F asked: "do you want me to shut it when you lie down or when I check you later?" She could not understand my reaction, telling me that she "checks" that all the children are sleeping well two or three times during the night! I explained that this would, most probably, lead the children to imagine that the night contained dangers that the mother was trying to protect them from. Mrs F was clearly embarrassed and said she would think about changing this routine.

Reference

Cain, A., & Cain, B. (1964). The replacement child. *Journal of the American Academy of Child and Adolescent Psychiatry*, *3*: 443–456.

CHAPTER FIVE

Unusual histories

I have found it difficult to define what exactly makes a life history "unusual". As will be seen, some of the following stories might be placed in other chapters of this book. They were included in this chapter because they contain not only an episode that I felt was interesting and unusual, but also presented features in the person's or the family's past history that were significant and not particularly obvious, that is, to a certain extent, "unusual".

Gabriel

This was a twelve-year-old boy who was presenting odd behaviour both at home and in the community. It was the school that decided the boy required a psychological assessment. An educational psychologist diagnosed psychotic behaviour and the boy was referred to the Child Guidance Clinic. Gabriel came to the consultation with his mother. Gabriel addressed me as any other normal boy of his age might do. But, as our conversation progressed, he told me that at times he would "see" distortions in people and things around him, and also have ideas that he knew were absurd "taking over" his thoughts, making him believe he was going crazy and this produced further intense anxious feelings.

He was seeing me with his mother. They came from an Oriental country and were devoted practitioners of their religion. They led a perfectly normal life, well settled into the local community. I was finding it quite difficult to make sense of Gabriel's "hallucinations", since his description of these appeared to be so discordant with the general picture of his personality. As our interview was coming to an end, the mother asked to see me on her own.

Mrs G wanted to tell me that her son's problems had started some months after his circumcision that had been performed, in line with their religious origins, some eight months earlier. After the surgical procedure, following the surgeon's recommendations, twice a day she would wash and clean the boy's prepuce and she had continued to perform this cleaning, even though she could see that the skin had healed perfectly. And she asked whether she was justified in continuing to do it. As gently as possible, I told her she should stop doing it.

Follow-up information was that the psychotic behaviour disappeared and when I offered another appointment, I was given their thanks but told that no further meetings were necessary.

This boy must have accepted that his mother considered the penis cleaning indispensable, while his mother believed that the original prescription had to be continued to ensure that there was no infection. The apparently psychotic symptoms probably expressed the boy's confusion when having to cope with feelings of fear, gratitude, sexual excitement, guilt, and resentment. The unconscious fantasies underlying his hallucinations were not uncovered, but the mother's change of approach was sufficient to stop the psychotic reaction of the young man.

Walter

The GP of the W family asked me to see this fifteen-year-old young man who was presenting serious behaviour problems both at school and at home. I saw him on his own and also with his parents. A charming youngster, clearly very intelligent, he could not sit still. He answered my questions in a friendly manner, but there was a sense of agitation or restlessness that kept him on the move all the time. One of Walter's teachers had accused him of unacceptable behaviour, but Walter refused to apologise to him.

Mr W was tall, thin, collected, almost frozen I thought. Mrs W sat comfortably, as if wanting to allow her husband and son to hold the floor. When I thought I had asked all the questions I wanted to put to them, I waited and, seeing they remained silent, I asked if they had anything to add. Parents remained silent, but eventually Walter said that the main problem was his temper and, after a brief pause, he added he had got it from his father. Mr W became simply furious. Trying to control himself, he spoke as if discussing an ordinary physical problem. He had joined temper control therapy, but he was not certain of how helpful it had been. Fortunately it did not seem to affect his professional persona, but he was aware of how his wife and children dreaded his losing control.

Mr W managed to tell me that on one occasion he had had a fight with Walter and when his son stopped, he had hit him on the head. Walter lost consciousness and had to be taken to hospital for X-rays. Mr W rounded off this account by saying that, luckily, that had been the only occasion when something so awful had happened. Walter corrected him and reminded him of another similar fight. Mr W tried to dismiss it, saying it had been a minor clash. But Walter had, obviously, felt supported by the consulting room atmosphere and went on to tell me that quite often his father will get angry and smash things around the house.

We were coming to the time when I had to stop our meeting and I said we had to discuss how to proceed. I told Walter and his parents that it was most important that he should have long-term individual psychotherapy and I urged them to see me again. I met them another couple of times and Walter did get a therapy vacancy in a psychotherapy organisation.

This family fits in perfectly with the English saying that the apple does not fall far from the apple tree, but from a scientific point of view, it would be fascinating to establish whether Walter learnt to be overactive and bound to loss of control due to the influence of the environment in which he grew up or whether he had some brain abnormality that would have led to this behaviour pattern whatever family he had been born in. But at the time I saw them, the 1980s, brain scans were not sophisticated enough to help us establish any underlying neurological pathology. We must, however, continue to hope that insight may lead an adolescent (and any adult) to learn how to deal with his aggressive feelings and change his approach to the world.

Rose

This thirty-four-year-old lawyer was born in South Asia and I only saw her for a few psychotherapy sessions. I wish to relate my findings here because not only was Rose an incredibly sensitive and competent person, but her life experiences represent such a dramatic picture of the culture into which she was born. I hope my notes are a correct rendering of Rose's account.

Rose had a sister, three years older than herself. When Rose was four months old she was sent off with a paternal aunt to live in a city many miles away from the family's home. This aunt was then in her mid-twenties; she had got married when she was thirteen years old, but her husband died seven years later. Rose loved this aunt with whom she lived for several years, without hearing anything from her parents. Suddenly, one night ("I remember it vividly", she said) her parents turned up unexpectedly and took Rose to yet another city, away from her aunt and away from their original family home.

Both Rose's parents were lawyers as is her older sister and one of her younger sisters, but the youngest daughter is an urban planner. I joked "she escaped", but Rose corrected me: "I saved her!"

Rose felt that her mother had treated her as a stepdaughter. When she was fifteen, she asked to move to a boarding school, claiming that she wanted to study, but in fact she was trying to "escape from (my) mother". She shared a room with another adolescent girl and they became very close friends. This girl would often break down in tears and Rose would console her. Eventually, this friend found a boyfriend whom she soon married—and Rose never heard from her again. Telling me of this episode, Rose went on to summarise what she felt was her life-long experience with the words "I just keep giving things to people, but never get anything back …"

Shortly after graduating from University, she met her husband. It turned out that both their mothers demanded that they should gain further professional experience in different parts of the country, which meant that it was only more than a year later that they were able to sign the marriage papers. Soon after this, the husband went off to another placement leaving Rose behind. Another year went by before the families held the official public marriage ceremony.

At last, this was the point at which they were entitled to have sex. But when they got to their new home, he told Rose that he would sleep in another room—and this set the pattern of their relationship. Those infrequent occasions when he joined Rose on her bed and tried to have sex, he would have a premature ejaculation and blame her for being too rigid. Surprisingly, she decided to have a hymenectomy, but this brought no change to their sexual life.

During one of these sexual encounters, Rose lost her temper and, much to her surprise, her husband did manage to penetrate and ejaculate. She said this was the one and only time they had full intercourse, but she got pregnant and eventually gave birth to a son.

The couple and their son moved to London. They had a comfortable flat, but slept in separate rooms. At some point, the husband agreed to consult a marriage counselling service. He not only showed his distress, but was also able to acknowledge it. Rose was convinced that he was not able to change his approach to her, but she said to me "The point is that I still love him!" Not long afterwards, however, she asked for "Khula" (a Muslim type of divorce that is initiated by the wife). This was granted and Rose went on to implement the three prescribed further steps that eventually led to an official divorce.

We were coming to the end of our consultation and much to my surprise Rose asked "Do you think I am being immoral?" I could only ask for an explanation. "Because I am talking to a stranger about family matters". I did not know what to say … I muttered my impression that all her conflicts were based on religion—correct? Rose explained, "I don't want to confront my mother … no point in seeking her approval … God is up there and he knows the truth." I said I was trying to understand her pain, not really judging her. She seemed more relaxed and when we arranged the date for a following meeting, she said "I will tell you more of my irrational things next time …"

At our next meeting Rose did tell me of further problems that I am not reporting here because they were part of daily, ordinary life and not really linked to any cultural factors. It was however interesting to learn that, other than myself, the one and only person with whom Rose had discussed her problems was her mother-in-law. When she told me this, my face could not hide my surprise … "I would not speak about my private life to friends or colleagues, because I would not fully trust them, but in our culture a mother will never breach confidence". But Rose was not prepared for what followed: only a few days later she heard from her parents that the mother-in-law had contacted them to say that Rose had let her son down, not trusting him as she should.

Rose came to see me a few more times. She was considering taking up a job in the Continent. She felt our sessions had helped her to feel less guilty of infringing the religious principles she had been brought up to follow. She smiled saying she did not see herself as "an ordinary" woman, since she felt that those religious beliefs were an integral part of her sense of self. However, she considered herself entitled to seek a new home in a different community.

Even if Rose considered her religious beliefs "part of (her) sense of self", it is still surprising and fascinating that she was able to recognise and act upon her private wishes. Rose classified her telling me of her problems as something "immoral" but she was also able to divorce her husband: we have two examples of a person claiming adherence to faith and still managing to claim her rights as an individual.

Lionel

I first saw this young man when he was twelve years old. I went on to see Lionel and his parents over several months. Time and again I would be told something that took me by surprise, making me wonder how was it possible that I had not learnt of it earlier.

The L family lived outside London. Two years before they contacted me, Lionel had suffered a virus infection and this triggered off episodes of panic, Lionel believing he was developing septicaemia or meningitis. Unfortunately, the same infection relapsed one year later and again Lionel complained of irrational anxieties. When Mrs L heard from Lionel's teachers that he seemed unhappy, always complaining that other boys did not like him and kept bullying him, she became afraid that Lionel might again be struggling with irrational fears. He was now twelve years old and she decided to seek help.

It was a friend of Mrs L's who gave her my name. The night before our meeting Mrs L had gone to Lionel's room to check whether he was doing his homework: he was, instead, watching TV and started to shout abuse at her and had nearly hit her. Fortunately, minutes later he came to the sitting room and apologised to his mother. Mrs L went on to tell me that this type of violence is typical of how her husband treats her.

However much Mrs L was concerned about Lionel being disrespectful and physically aggressive, she was more worried about him showing signs of irrationality, even "madness". She clearly struggled when making herself tell me that she had accused her husband of passing on to Lionel the genes affecting his family. He responded telling her that her family's genes were no better than his.

Mrs L was in her early fifties and was a very successful financial advisor. Her parents' marriage was "dreadful—fights day and night". Mrs L had got married in her early thirties and, like her husband, she did not want to have children. Seeing the forties approaching, she changed her mind and soon gave birth to Lionel and, two years later, to his younger sister. But looking after the children proved a major stress and she became what she called "hyper"—"I would not call it a breakdown ..." but not long afterwards she decided to stop work so as to look after the children.

Mr L was the same age as his wife. A senior IT expert, he came from a large family, whose members were very successful in their careers, but a large number of them led horrendously unhappy lives and also had many cases of severe psychiatric illness.

When I met Lionel and his parents, Mrs L told me that when they had decided to have a child, she had had a miscarriage and then nearly miscarried Lionel's younger sister. Lionel jumped: he had not known of this and, with a very disturbed voice said: "quite scary to think that I might never have been here—or, worse still, be in my sister's place!"

I was told of how Lionel loses control and is too "big-headed", "cannot bear boys who are not intelligent". In spite of these accounts, considering other things Lionel told us, I voiced my impression that he tries to say what he believes others want to hear. Mr L showed his surprise and said this is not how he thinks of Lionel, but the boy went on to give examples of his anxiety of upsetting others.

Our meeting was moving to an end and we had a much more peaceful, friendlier atmosphere in the room. We arranged to meet some weeks later and Mr L responded very positively to my suggestion that he should try to discuss with Lionel how they could improve their relationship. Mrs L had a very pleased and proud smile on her face as she followed their conversation.

I met Mr and Mrs L again three weeks later. They felt Lionel had shown great progress in his behaviour and especially in his relationship to the two of them. But Mr L now voiced his anxiety about Joyce, Lionel's younger sister. She would lose her temper without any sign that this might occur. It was over this, and what emerged in the following two meetings, that it became clear that Mrs L had serious concerns about Joyce's mental state. I learnt that Joyce would wake up in the middle of the night and join her mother in her bed—and this led to the revelation that for quite some time Mr L had been sleeping on his own in a separate bedroom. When I next saw Lionel, I learnt that he was familiar with this night-time scenario: in fact, he often woke up and went round the house checking where each one was …

Some weeks later, Lionel told me of his fear that he might be developing septicaemia: he showed me a cut on his arm and another cut on his knee. What surprised me was Lionel telling me that the moment his mother saw these cuts, she promptly put iodine on them and made an appointment with the family's GP to enquire whether Lionel should have antibiotics. This led me to suggest to Lionel that when he next got worried about his body/mind state, he should look back, look around, and check whether he had spotted any sign of his mother being worried. He smiled, making it clear that this comment of mine did not really surprise him.

Two months later, Mrs L phoned and asked me to see her. She felt at the end of her tether, worried she might have a nervous breakdown. Mrs L felt she could no longer remain a part of the marriage. Struggling with very painful feelings, she told me that they had not had any further sex since the birth of Joyce. She did not mind this so much, and it was her husband's detachment, crudeness, aggressiveness, and violence that she wanted to get away from. Predictably, she added that she had remained married "for the sake of the children".

I went on seeing Lionel and his parents for several months and after we stopped I met them again one year later. As the French saying goes, "*plus ça change, plus ça change pas*". Lionel had become a very tall adolescent and was enjoying a successful life at a prestigious secondary school—but his anxieties kept bouncing to the surface from time to time. His parents continued their stormy relationship and Joyce had become querulous and aggressive, but still keeping company in bed with her mother, while Mr L had continued to sleep on his own.

Donald

This gentleman came to see me so that his health insurance would cover his psychotherapy with a non-medical colleague of mine. I was amazed to have in front of me a totally normal looking man in his early fifties who recounted a life marked with repeated traumas that might have devastated other human beings. After my consultation he went back to his therapist and I had no further news, but I decided to include his history here because it is a precious example of human resilience—and persistence. Or, as some of my colleagues would say, of masochism.

Starting from an ordinary working class background, Donald had made his way to become a senior, successful university teacher. He had a younger sister, who was now married and looking after her children and grandchildren. Donald described his mother as "terrible", tyrannical and always complaining of body troubles. He adored his father and was immensely upset when, after a fall, his father was diagnosed with MS, eventually dying when Donald was in his mid-twenties. For reasons I could not really understand, Donald and his sister wanted their mother to sell her house and move to a flat. Mother refused to do it but they carried on with the selling process. When the day came that final papers would be signed, Mother overdosed and died.

Donald got married soon after finishing his studies, and not surprisingly, married a lady who was a serious hypochondriac, as his mother had been. Not long after marriage, Donald discovered his wife was having an affair with a friend of theirs, but he decided to ignore it. Years went by and when Donald had an affair with a lady colleague, his wife decided they should divorce. This was when Donald started his psychotherapy. One day he discovered a new woman, Helen, and started a relationship where he found "amazing, lovely sex", embarking on a closer relationship even after learning that she had taken two overdoses after the failure of earlier affairs.

Helen had three children from two marriages, all of whom hated Donald. She had one brother who abused her throughout her childhood and apparently one of her fathers-in-law had also managed to seduce her during some holidays.

Donald was obviously determined to find some positive solution, some step that would make Helen have a normal, married, relationship with him. Carefully choosing my words, I told him that his account gave me the impression that he felt very insecure and anxious about Helen's capacity to lead a smooth, "normal" life, but even so I was left with the feeling that he was unable to stop, get out of situations that caused him pain. Donald went on to tell me that he had tried to find other women, but now discovered that he could not reach an erection. This led him to a conviction that only Helen enabled him to be potent. I could not resist pointing out that chances were that if he found himself enjoying company and sex with another woman, this would put an end to his involvement with Helen. Surprisingly, he smiled, saying that I was probably right …

I urged him to continue his therapy.

Baker

Mr Baker was in his fifties when he came to see me at the recommendation of a friend of his, who believed I would be able to help him. It happens that some years later Mrs Baker urged their son, Chris, to consult me. He only attended for two meetings, but several years later he asked me for a new consultation. I found these meetings fascinating. Of course it is a common saying that "the apple does not fall far from the apple tree" and, indeed, psychoanalysts are great believers in the influence of parental input on the development of the individual. But the manner in which Mr Baker and his son addressed me and the way in which they described their experience of family and ordinary daily life left me wondering how attitudes and emotional relations could be reproduced, duplicated to such an extent and in such a dramatic manner.

Mr Baker's parents had a daughter who died of epilepsy when she was seven years old. They were immensely upset by this loss and Mr Baker remembers being told by his mother that his birth several years after the girl's death "had been a mistake". Mr Baker himself only got married after his thirtieth birthday. He felt happy with his wife, but found difficulties in their sexual life. He enjoyed this side of their life, but gradually this changed and it was his wife who decided when they could have sex. Sadly, she gave birth to twins and one of them died *in utero*. Mr Baker gradually developed a position of coldness and detachment that he attributed to his wife's behaviour, but in our consultation I found that this emotional façade also had other causes. Mr Baker also told me of an aunt taking him every year to visit his dead sister's grave, but he claimed to have no feelings about her death: exactly the same as his "no feelings" reaction to the death of his own child.

I met Chris, Mr Baker's son, when he was thirty. He was a successful lawyer and lived on his own. He described his father as "very closed in, loving, but never shows or talks of feelings." He said his mother "had a miserable life, but she is very loving". His picture was of a family where nobody knew how anybody else *really* felt. They never talked of sex or anything linked to relationships. Chris had had some girlfriends, but only at age twenty-seven did he first have sex. He continued the relationship with this girl for a year, but then they broke off.

I was struck by Chris' constraint. It was "hard work" to draw him out and I thought he lacked any sense of humour, there was no colouring to his words. And his account of his relationships with women led me to ask if he had any negative feelings about his sexuality. He seemed relieved to acknowledge his feeling of dissatisfaction with his sexual performance. But also important was my impression that Chris had no reaction at all to being praised or valued by friends or colleagues.

We had a few meetings and Chris decided to stop, since he was assigned to a job abroad. He contacted me again some years later: nothing had changed in his life. He was successful at work and led an active social life, but his relationship to women was unchanged. He told me about his parents' clashes: mother would shout at father, but the latter remained controlled, collected. I thought Chris was very attached to his mother, but his presentation was exactly, precisely the same as his description of his father's attitude to people and life. He knew that a twin brother had died, but this was an event about which he claimed not to have any feelings. In spite of this denial, I was certain that this event had enormous influence on his relationship to women—friendship, sex: fine, but procreation was to be avoided.

I was puzzled to see the similarity of the reaction that father and son had to learning that a sibling of theirs had died. As described in other cases in this book, learning of such an event tends to lead to an emotional experience of "not entitlement" to the fulfilment of their potentials. Chris and Mr Baker had built a façade of "emotional closure" to the world and Chris seemed quite aware of his reluctance to impregnate a woman. I was left with the feeling that, however understandable, it was still most remarkable to find that death, loss, had always been a taboo subject in this family.

Vivien

This lady was in her early forties when she came to see me. She was worried about her daughter, aged six at the time and also involved in conflict with her ex-husband who wanted to have closer involvement with their daughter. Vivien had a very complex life history and the reason for describing her story is the manner in which she dealt with the woman who brought her into the world: she forgave her and engaged with her.

Vivien was brought up as an adopted child. Her mother had been only thirteen years old when she gave birth to Vivien and was not allowed to look after her. Vivien grew up with Saul, four years older than her, also adopted by the same couple. The two were never very close, though they played and worked well together. Saul did not mind being adopted and was now married and had two children.

When she was twenty years old, Vivien made enquiries and discovered her biological mother: she had had two more children with the same man, but had kept and brought up both of them—however, soon after the children started attending school, the couple divorced. Vivien remained in close contact with mother and siblings.

Vivien always dreamt of travelling and when she was in her early twenties she went to South America to work in a firm connected to her adoptive father. There she met Jonas: they fell in love and he joined her when she returned to the UK several years later. Vivien stopped taking the contraceptive pill and soon became pregnant. During the pregnancy Jonas developed a multitude of psychosomatic illnesses and when Fanny was born the relationship fell apart. Telling me this, Vivien burst out laughing and said that she just could not make sense of the fact that he had followed her into the delivery room but soon after her coming home he had "gone off sex". It was only three years before seeing me that they formally divorced and Jonas "went to pieces", rushing off to find and marry another woman.

Now Vivien and Jonas were clashing over custody. They had bought their house with Vivien's money, but she still gave him sixty per cent of its value, so that he could buy a place for himself. Jonas and Saul were helping Vivien's adoptive mother with her business, but Vivien chose to build her own business in marketing.

Fanny was developing very normally, happy, and healthy. Vivien went on to have a three year relationship with a colleague, got engaged, but then realised he "was dreadful" and broke the engagement off. An interesting detail: Vivien repeated several times her preoccupation to help Fanny become independent and learn to look after herself "before she is thirteen", but was surprised and burst out laughing when I called her attention to the fact that this was her mother's age when giving birth to her.

Robert

This is one of those cases that will feed passionate debates about the role of early experiences in the development of the individual's personality. Robert had seen a couple of psychotherapists in the past and had only decided to consult me in order to please his wife who apparently insisted it might make him "a happier man".

Robert was in his late forties. A successful lawyer, he had two children who seemed to be moving happily and successfully in their adult lives. The relationship with his wife had always presented problems and they had seen a marital therapist for a while. Periods of peace did occur, but Robert's wife had gone through periods of depression that led her to seek individual psychotherapy help.

Robert was a tall, elegant, articulate gentleman, who was clearly self-conscious and ill at ease when seeing me. I thought he looked Jewish and when telling me of his family history he mentioned that only in his twenties had he "discovered" that his father was Jewish—though he had never made contact with Jewish communities. Indeed, in spite of complex and recurring events and discussions throughout his life, religion or ethnical origin meant just nothing to Robert. Even if occasionally feeling depressed, his sense of self seemed not to contain doubts or anxieties. I believe Robert was happy with my questions and comments, because he seemed to relax and allow a degree of "warmth" to surface. He told me some stories about his children and this led him to mention events of his own childhood that I would never have been able to guess.

When Robert was two and a half years old he developed "mastoids" (sic) and was admitted to the local hospital, where he stayed for *five* months! He did not have any recollection of this event, but he does remember being told that one day he was crying so much that the nurses locked him in a cabinet. He smiled when seeing my expression of surprise and horror at such cruelty. He went on to add that when he was eight years old he had a recurrence of the problem and was kept as an in-patient for *two* months.

We discussed how to proceed and Robert told me, very gently, that he wanted time to think about our meeting before making a decision. He wrote to me two weeks later, thanking me for my input, but saying he preferred not to start regular therapy at that point.

Meeting someone like Robert and taking into account their appearance, style of relating and learning of the emotional experiences of his childhood, adolescence and adult life, how does one decide what role did his illnesses play on shaping his adult self?

Gregory

This gentleman was in his early sixties when he came to see me. He held a senior position in an important art gallery and anyone who knew him would be convinced that this was a successful, happy man who led an active, enjoyable life. Sadly, this was not his private emotional experience. Over the years he had seen various therapists, but never found any significant change in his experience of life. I saw Gregory for a few months and we stopped when he felt we had gone as far as he believed we could go.

Gregory had had periods of drinking too much and was always worried about what he might have said when drunk. But he had completely stopped drinking several years before seeing me. He had been involved in several serious relationships and had a son who was engaged in a successful and promising career in the IT world. Gregory told me of his family life: his father was in his eighties when he died of lung cancer. Gregory's mother died of thrombosis when he was nine years old and I was puzzled to learn that he had never checked on her death certificate or with family relatives, to learn of what had precipitated the thrombosis. But he experienced very strong feelings all through his life because of not being allowed to attend her funeral. I was surprised when he went on to tell me that this chapter of "death" held a further instance: many years earlier he had been told that his parents had had a daughter who had been ran over and killed by a car when she was seven years old. Again, Gregory had never asked questions about this event, but when I indicated my surprise about his "silence" he commented in a heavy, sad voice: "I've been the unlucky one … I grew up and all the faults came out …"

Gregory told me about medieval books stating that there are two kinds of death: the rich die but the poor disappear. He was clearly haunted, tormented by his lack of memories of life during his childhood and early adolescence. I decided to tell him about children not believing someone had *really* died when they had not been allowed to see the corpse or attend the burial. His face showed an expression of surprise and, with difficulty, he told me of a memory: when he was about ten years old, he used to go and return from school quite convinced that his father had hidden his mother somewhere, so that she was alive—and he would choose ever differing routes, hoping that one day he would find her!

Mark

This gentleman was in his late thirties when he came to see me. He had had therapy in the past and had now applied to have therapy at a training organisation that asked me to assess his suitability for psychotherapy by a trainee. He felt unhappy and dissatisfied with his position in life; occasionally he did consider the word "depressed" and he had moments when he questioned the purpose of living. However, he was only too aware of how successful he was in his professional life, with family, friends, and colleagues praising his creativity and this encouraged him to seek help.

Mark's account of his life contained no end of experiences that were bound to affect a person's development. He remembered his father bathing him and when drying him putting him in a position where he was lying on his abdomen and on his bent knees—and after a few minutes of watching Mark, father would leave the bathroom and return shortly afterwards. At some point in his teens Mark found himself compulsively cleaning his bottom and he realised that his father must have been masturbating while watching him.

Mark's mother had always had a very fragile personality. Several members of her family had suffered from psychiatric disorders and some deaths had occurred in puzzling circumstances. But the episode that most intrigued me was his mother telling Mark that a dramatic turning point had occurred when he was three years old and she took him to a shop to buy shoes. She felt she had always been "normal", but from the moment they left that shop she had become depressed—for the rest of her life. How are we supposed to evaluate this recollection? How can we establish its importance in that child's development?

Mark had come to see his relationships with women as following a pattern he had been unable to change. He had a girlfriend for four years and this came to an end when he engaged in an affair with a newly found lady; he had another relationship with a married lady who then decided to re-engage with her husband; he went on to enter another relationship that broke off when he again started an affair. But most strikingly, he had continued to sustain a friendly relationship with every one of these women. His summing-up of this pattern was moving and eloquent: "I somehow seem to have a need for two people at the same time!"

I recommended Mark for a vacancy at the training organisation.

Helen

What follows is what I was told by this lady when she consulted me after being urged by a friend to seek psychotherapy to relieve her state of unhappiness and anxiety. She was clearly not keen to pursue such an enterprise, but somehow seemed to need to share with me her view of what life had brought her way.

Helen's mother's family were Sephardi Jews who migrated from Spain to India at the time of the Inquisition. They became "pillars of society" and her mother's great-grandfather became a Chief Rabbi. Maternal grandmother gave birth to Helen's mother and three years later she had a son. It happened that seven years later she died of peritonitis after a burst appendix, but she was eight months pregnant at that point. Helen was told that an "even number of children cannot survive" and this meant that the newborn boy was left in a corner for three days until he died of starvation. Over the years Helen had consulted many people about this "belief" and every single person had denied this had ever been known to exist—nevertheless, Helen could not avoid having this memory as part of her life experiences.

Helen told me of another belief: when eight years old she had watched a film where the main artist's mother had died at age fifty-four and Helen became convinced that her aunt (who had played a major role in Helen's upbringing) would also die at fifty-four and, furthermore, that she, Helen, herself would also die at age fifty-four. In fact this aunt had died at age ninety-two, not long before Helen came to see me.

Helen's father had also gone through several countries before settling in India. He was a successful businessman, but "privately was a depressed, sadistic brute" who had many affairs. Mother had not opposed this behaviour. When dying at age eighty-three, father's last words were "so good that we stayed together!"

Helen told me of a staggering series of physical illnesses, but while being a "fascinating medical case", and finding doctors and nurses being praised for their achievements, she felt, herself, totally ignored as a suffering youngster. At one point she developed "a kind of polio" and was kept on a bed for eight months! Not only "lying on a bed", because nurses objected to her attempts at movement and proceeded to tie her down in complex ways.

Helen had married a man and they had two daughters. But she divorced him after seven years and since that point, she had engaged in relationships that, sooner or later, led to conflicts and separation. She did not enjoy living on her own or having her daughters living with her, neither could she convince herself that she might still find a good, loving, supporting partner. "I am driven to unreliable men!" was her assessment.

I urged Helen to have psychotherapy, but I had no follow-up to our meeting.

Bridget

This is another example of a person who can identify the traumatic experiences that coloured his/her life and nevertheless finds that time and again they are driven to develop closer relationships with people who, sooner or later, behave in a manner that brings to the surface the same experience of being hurt and rendered defenceless.

Bridget was in her early forties when she approached a psychotherapy society, hoping they would offer her a therapy vacancy. She had three older siblings who had achieved reasonable success in their professional life, though they had gone through repeated sequences of marriage, divorce, and new attempts at forming a family. Like her siblings, she was facing repeated failed attempts to achieve stability, continuity.

Bridget's mother came from a middle class family. Her father was a lawyer and had died only a few months before our assessment interview, after a painful physical and mental deterioration. Bridget had been very attached to him, describing him as always supportive, "a very sweet nature man". Her mother was still alive, but also facing illnesses. Bridget said that throughout her life, mother would provoke father until he lost control and hit her. "But he never hit unprovoked!" was her "redeeming" addendum. It happened, however, that the children were often hitting each other and a brother had hit the father as well. "A very violent family, unfortunately ..."

Bridget met George on holiday and when both decided to live together, he joined her in London. It happened that he had no definite profession and Bridget undertook to cover his expenses. However much Bridget loved George, she was clear that marriage or children were out of the question. She felt that their personalities were dramatically different and, even if she knew that she was being exploited, she insisted that she loved him and she was willing to let him carry on in his way. He was happy with this and they lived together for five years, when unexpectedly he accepted an offer of a job in the Continent—and left.

Some months later she met Harry and soon he moved in to her flat. This was a man who was prepared to share a sexual life, but otherwise carried on his business interests. He could become argumentative and verbally aggressive, but Bridget was prepared to accept this.

When he suddenly announced he was moving out, Bridget found herself profoundly depressed and soon started to contemplate suicide. She described the various techniques she considered and recounted how she ended up swallowing a large amount of Paracetamol and other tablets she had at home. Fortunately, a friend happened to call in and Bridget was taken to hospital, where she was kept for two nights.

When I asked how she saw the future, she shook her shoulders and muttered "nothing, really …" I thought I had to ask her if she still considered suicide. Bridget said with a self-deprecatory tone of voice "if so, then I'll throw myself from a high enough building …" It was quite clear that, however much pain Bridget experienced, as soon as she was addressing another person, a touch of humour coloured her words and her expression. She was aware of this and she stated how much she valued speaking to "somebody intelligent and interested", but as soon as a more formal, intimate relationship was contemplated, Bridget had a clear image in her mind: "it is two people forming a unit—and if one moves away, the other is reduced to a living half …" I thought this was an insightful summing-up: Bridget was not happy living on her own and this led her to seek a partner—but however comforting this could be, she seemed aware of some unconscious drive that led her to choose men who eventually threw her back into solitude: the same helplessness she had experienced in her childhood. I did recommend the psychotherapy society to offer Bridget a vacancy.

Susan

This lady was in her early fifties when she came to see me for psychotherapy. She proved to be one more of those people who make me wonder about the truth of their accounts of childhood experiences and the significance of these events/memories in determining the course of their adult life. I am well aware of our formulation that memories are remembered and perhaps expressed in tune with our specific mood at that point in time—and that it is not necessarily the case that they render actual early experiences. Susan, however, was one more of those people who told me of experiences that I could not doubt stemmed from actual events.

Susan was a senior social worker who worked in several clinics and hospitals. A distinguished and highly qualified professional, she had a warm and friendly appearance. She spoke in a quiet, calm way but her words could convey extremely painful feelings. When we first met she told me of being worried about the hatred and murderousness she was experiencing.

Susan was born two years after a brother had died in a car accident when he was six years old. Before Susan's birth, her mother had suffered a miscarriage. Her father was a skilled builder who travelled a lot and sometimes took Susan with him—and she had happy memories of these trips together with her father. But he was despised and tormented by his wife: colossal rows occurred and one day when they moved to a smaller flat, father was banished to one of the rooms, and Susan, then in her teens, slept with mother on the same bed. She described her mother as violent, horrible, and temperamental.

Susan's father died of a heart attack when she was at University. Her mother was incapacitated by rheumatism and became increasingly dependent on Susan. It was many years before Susan managed to muster the courage to move to her own flat, but a routine developed where she was supposed to telephone her mother every morning and evening, besides spending weekends at her mother's flat. And what followed may sound like a work of fiction: one day Susan phoned her mother and apologised that she would not be able to come to her place on Saturday because she had a work party she could not fail to attend, but she would certainly come over on Friday. And when she got to the mother's flat on Friday night, Susan found her mother had committed suicide having taken a lot of tablets.

Time and again Susan would tell me of thoughts that made me feel the urge to question and perhaps correct her. A striking example came when she told me of her professional graduation and that her first job was in a prison—and she took this as evidence of her murderousness. Exaggerated, to say the least—and yet I had to respect it as true.

Susan had many colleagues and friends, but only two or three times had she succeeded in forming a closer relationship with a man: and each of them turned out to be selfish and cold towards her. Before coming to see me, Susan had seen a couple of therapists, one of which had been very helpful but decided to retire after a period of time.

Susan also told me of two members of her circle of friends who had committed suicide. Her work exposed her to endless number of severely ill psychiatric patients and it was not surprising that suicides should upset her, when this had been how her mother had died. And here I would add another memory Susan carried with her: there were many, many occasions when her mother would cry, complain of the way Susan was treating her and adding that her dead son would have treated her more kindly.

My summary: Susan was not suicidal, her reactions to suicide varied between coldness and panic—but the way in which she had been born and lived engulfed by death had probably led her to feel as if not yet entitled to take advantage of the fact of being alive.

I saw Susan for some months and she came to see me again some time later. She felt less anxious, led a more active social life, but her work still kept her involved with severely ill patients.

Alain

This French gentleman was in his early forties when he came to see me. A highly regarded IT specialist, he was puzzled by the fact that, however successful and praised, he remained incapable of enjoying, savouring, experiencing himself as successful—he would compulsively find himself facing doubts, questions, suspicions of not having reached the desired goal. He had seen psychoanalysts in the past, but the problem had not been solved.

Alain came from a very unusual background. His father was a successful industrialist and brought up his family in a village not far from Bordeaux. Alain's mother devoted herself to look after the house and the family. She had two daughters and went on to have two miscarriages. But Mr A was obsessed with having a son and decided to adopt a boy who had been brought to France from one of its African ex-colonies. Mr A was jubilant and doted on this boy, whom he saw as the fulfilment of his dreams. And it happened that three years later Mrs A gave birth to Alain.

Alain recounted an extremely painful childhood. Even if his successful social and school life was in marked contrast to his brother's endless troubles, Alain was virtually ignored by his father and saw himself gradually coming closer and closer to his elder sisters. Could this perhaps have been a factor in his doubting his sexual identity when reaching puberty? He found himself attracted to both young men and young women, continuously struggling to define his sexual self.

Alain was in his early thirties when he met Suzanne and, by the time he came to see me, they had been married for some six years. Very happy together, Alain felt his sexual identity conflicts moving out of his life. But new problems emerged. Suzanne suffered a tubal pregnancy and a series of treatments were required before she gave birth to their son. Alain clearly loved and felt proud of his growing son.

However, Alain's sense of dissatisfaction persisted. He felt that all his life he had come through first in exams and competitions, but this left him with an overwhelming feeling of guilt and anxiety. He gave me a very insightful reading of his problem: "Perhaps I am competing with my brother—failing and not engaging in celebrations, so as to be the same source of trouble as he was and perhaps gaining some attention from my father".

We discussed further meetings, but Alain learnt that his company was moving him to a city out of London.

I see Alain as an unusual presentation of the "replacement child" syndrome. A deep, prevailing sense of non-entitlement that repeatedly spoils any achievement. His problems with sexual identity also seem to stem from the dynamics of his environment, rather than from any hormonal or neurological structure. His sisters loved and valued him, but even if he was a male like his adopted brother, his father still ignored him—could it be that "copying" his sisters would have been an unconscious attempt to obtain the same love from father as they had?

Maurice

This young man was in his late twenties when he came to see me. He was struggling to complete his PhD work and, as had happened many times in his adult life, he was desperately trying to sort out his relationship with a woman. This time this involved his wife, but the same thing had happened in the past with other women and, in fact, with women he met while he and the wife were living apart. From his accounts, he seemed to have no trouble in captivating young ladies, but after a while he felt some compulsion to break up the relationship, while paradoxically he would increase his attempts to please them. This led him to great difficulties in falling asleep and episodes of crippling anxiety.

Maurice was very articulate and in a curious way he would often resort to images to convey his thoughts with full clarity. One example was his trying to convey the puzzling "mystery" of his efforts to make sense of the ideas that clogged up his mind and impeded him from falling asleep: he referred to the globe-like bulbs of the street lights that existed in the city of his childhood. Yes, he knew there must be a lamp inside, but he would spend hours trying to figure out what else might those balls contain. My psychoanalytic framework led me to thoughts of pregnancy and I knew that Maurice was an only child but I did not feel this was the time to ask about his birth.

One day, Maurice was describing the type of trouble that surfaced whenever he would take his wife to a restaurant: she was obsessed with eating pizzas, something he hated. I commented that he was again referring to the already many times mentioned fear of causing pain or disappointment. He paused for a while and then, with a tone of voice suggesting he had doubts about my response to his words, he said "truly, this is like a mother feeding her baby—and the baby knowing that he must continue to suck her breast to keep her alive ... because if he stops ... what can the mother do?" So, I asked him for whose sake does the baby continue to suck the breast? To make sure he has food available? To please the mother? Is there a fear that mother will not survive? And Maurice smiled: "Well ... it is really difficult to know, isn't it?"

Maurice had described his mother as emotionally very unstable—"sometimes she would hide away in her bedroom for one or two days." But "she was all the time watching what I did and what I said, often correcting me." Another day Maurice told me that his memories of early childhood involved his being in the company of a nanny, who looked after him until he started to attend primary school. It happened one day, when he was about ten years old, that his mother spoke about seeing her analyst. "I plucked up my courage and asked her why she had analysis and she answered that 'if it was not for (my) analysis, I would never have managed to get married or to have a child.' I felt devastated! I thought that if not for the analysis, I would not have been born".

I do believe that the pattern Maurice developed in his relationships with women in adult life was unconsciously determined by his ideas of wanting/being wanted, needing/being needed, not wanting/not being wanted he felt had operated between him and his mother.

Maurice did manage to divorce his wife, but when he finished his PhD he went back to his country of origin. I am sure he sought further analysis when he got there.

Giselle

This lady was in her early fifties when she asked to see me, to discuss some problems she was not managing to sort out. She knew a couple of my colleagues who suggested she contacted me. She was happy to tell me about her life that contained no end of unusual and unexpected developments.

Giselle was born in the West Country and had an older brother. Somehow, her mother loved that son and simply hated Giselle, whom she would hit mercilessly whenever she lost her temper. Father never intervened. When she was ten years old her brother started to invite her to his bed and she masturbated him. One day he jumped on her, she panicked fearing she might get pregnant and told her mother what had happened. Mother was furious with her son and this brother never spoke to Giselle again. She could tell me another puzzling story: she had a violent teacher who caned her "all the time". She never reported him to anyone, but some years later she learnt that he had murdered his wife. A "funny" touch came when Giselle decided to move to London—her father had never given signs of knowing that his wife beat Giselle, but now he said to her that, because of her departure, he would be at the receiving end of the wife's temper …

Giselle found it very difficult to settle in London. She tried living with a cousin, then with a friend, she went to several courses and only after a few years did she discover that she enjoyed working with people, whereupon she embarked on a counselling course. She had gone through several relationships, but only in her early forties did she find the man she came to marry. She met him at some friends' party and got attracted to him, even if knowing that he had no work or living place. She must have played an important role in his life, since he took a couple of courses and became quite an expert in his work. However, Giselle felt he never "looked after her", so that she often felt lonely. And if any friend asked "any children?" Giselle would name her husband as the child she looked after …

Summing-up my views regarding her account, I put it to Giselle that she was repeatedly finding men who took advantage of her kindness and ability to help, look after and gratify them—but it seemed that other than comply with these demands, she only imagined herself replicating her mother's violent temper, a possibility that clearly scared her. She had tears in her eyes, "very true"—and this is why she was feeling depressed and had consulted her GP, who wanted her to take anti-depressants. Giselle lived too far from me and I offered to find a colleague near her home, who might take her on for therapy. She thanked me, saying our meeting had been helpful, but she wanted to think about it all, before embarking on therapy.

CHAPTER SIX

Sentences

This is a collection of phrases that impressed me by the clarity, sharpness, richness of meaning encapsulated in their few words. They all come from interviews that lasted over one hour. Each person had his own style of expressing himself—some were verbose, others monosyllabic, some were comfortable conveying their feelings and experiences in minute details, others restricted themselves to concise answers to my questions: no end of variations. But every now and again I would hear a few words that "spoke volumes". This fascinated me and I decided to share these gems.

John P

John P was a very disturbed sixteen-year-old young man struggling with alcohol, drugs, and multiple conflicts with friends. However intelligent and academically successful in earlier years, he was now unable to turn his potentials for success into reality. At times he could feel suicidal, but he "reassured" me that this was unlikely to happen. As we discussed details of his life, we came to focus on his family relationships and he put into words a sentiment that I had met many times, but never so sharply formulated: "my parents love me as their son, not as me".

I believe that John's feelings are pretty much the same as those described by Roger (see below) and by Patrick J (see Chapter Four "Interesting stories"). These are children who feel, or try to feel, that they are loved by one or both parents and yet time and again find that the parent(s) show no interest in their thoughts and feelings. From an outsider's point of view, these are parents who never ask questions, concentrating instead on giving advice or demanding discipline. Many of these parents sincerely believe (as did Roger's father) that they are being helpful and protective, but this is definitely not what the child experiences.

Roger

I had seen Mr R for individual psychotherapy quite a few times, though never for regular sessions. One day he asked me to see his son, aged thirteen. They came together and Roger chose to have his father present while we talked. This was clearly a very intelligent and articulate young man, well able to answer my questions. Roger told me that he was finding it extremely difficult to fall asleep, being overwhelmed by thoughts that made him very anxious. "How long has this been the case?" I asked. "Something like five months ago" he answered. I asked, "Do you have any idea of what could have brought this about?" "Yes", he said, "that was the time when my paternal grandfather died ... I was very close to him and he died very suddenly". It turned out that this was not the first loss that Roger had experienced. Earlier this meeting, I had been told that some four years earlier Mrs R, his mother, had died, only a few months after surgery for ovarian cancer.

It was very clear that Roger had been immensely affected by his mother's illness and death. He was trying hard to find the words to convey how vivid were his feelings of loss and guilt, because he felt he had not done enough to comfort his mother. But Mr R was increasingly upset by his son's painful feelings and began to speak, trying to console Roger. I stopped him and asked him to allow Roger to continue.

When Roger came to a pause, I decided to ask him if he knew why I had stopped his father from speaking. I never expected the answer he gave me: "because if he comforted me, I would feel that he is not interested in learning how I, myself, feel about it".

Would anyone ever guess what Roger's answer would be? After we discussed his feelings further, I had to stop the interview and we made an appointment for a follow-up meeting, but his father telephoned to cancel it, telling me that since our discussion, Roger had been much more relaxed and now able to fall asleep without difficulty. However, even if not seeing Roger again, I fear that there was no change in the dynamics of his relationship with his father.

Mr and Mrs D

I had seen Mrs D individually for several months and, at her suggestion, I went on to see her together with her husband for weekly sessions. Both were in their mid-forties and they had been married for nearly twenty years. Mr D was a successful businessman, they had three adolescent children and, by all accounts, they had a peaceful, successful, social and family life. I knew from my meetings with Mrs D that she had refused to have sex since the birth of her youngest child, and I am reporting this couple because at one point, when we were discussing Mr D's frequent travels abroad, Mrs D accused him, quite bitterly, of meeting prostitutes when travelling. Considering the supposedly harmonious *modus vivendi* of their ordinary life, I was surprised by her words and the anger in her voice. I wondered how Mr D would deal with this accusation, but I could not guess how he responded to his wife. His face showed anger, but his voice had a touch of humour, as he seemed to address himself to me: "If my wife does not give me food, am I expected to die of hunger?" I did not entirely succeed in my attempt not to smile. Mrs D was obviously angry and upset, but I was quite convinced that they would continue to live together—which they did.

Serge

This nine-year-old boy was referred to the Child Guidance Clinic because of behaviour in classes and in the playground that his teachers felt demanded professional assessment. Serge came to see me with his parents. Mr S had a job in town and Mrs S was a housewife, devoted to the upbringing of Serge and his younger sister. Both parents seemed to feel quite at ease and Serge was, at my request, making a drawing. Mrs S was telling me about the family history and at one point she said that, some time before Serge's birth, she had suffered a miscarriage. Serge stopped drawing and faced his mother with an expression of obviously disturbed surprise. He uttered some words like, "Really?!

Do you mean …?!" I asked him if this was the first time he had heard of this event. Mr and Mrs S were puzzled by their son's reaction and asked him what this could mean to him.

Like the parents, I was also wondering what Serge would answer. He had a reflective expression on his face, clearly searching for the words and, after a little while, he said, slowly and quietly: "Well … it is strange … it is the thought that if that child had been born, I might never have been born myself …"

This was not the only occasion that I heard this comment when a child first learnt of similar circumstances preceding their birth. One of these must be quoted, since it raises the complex discussions on the issue of adoption. This was a seven-year-old adopted boy who was presenting behaviour problems that led to his referral to me. I was seeing him together with his mother, who, as it happens, had gone on to give birth to two children. One day this lady brought all three children to our meeting and, as I had a new social worker in the room, she introduced them to her: "My adopted son Darrell and these are Mary and John." Darrell could not contain himself and protested to his mother: "Must you really mention all the time that I was adopted?" When I saw them another time, some weeks later, his mother was giving me a more detailed account of her life and came to tell me that soon after marriage she had given birth to a child who died a few days later—and it was soon afterwards that she decided to adopt a boy. Darrell was very shocked and, with a trembling voice, said: "So if that child had not died, I would not have been adopted …"

Charles[1]

The paediatrician referred this sixteen-year-old young man to me. Charles suffered from bed-wetting and urinary urgency and many tests and consultations had failed to discover any physical abnormality in his genito-urinary system. Various drugs and endless advice had all failed to affect his complaint. Charles came with his parents to our consultation. I am quoting it here because of Charles' reaction when, to his surprise and amazement, he realised how his symptoms had appeared and persisted.

Mr and Mrs C described how their family outings were repeatedly interrupted by Charles' request to find a toilet. Daily family life and school hours followed the same pattern. And Charles confirmed these stories, clearly pained and ashamed of his helplessness vis-à-vis his symptom. He was totally convinced that there was some organic abnormality in his urinary system. Because this was an intelligent secondary school student, I asked him what he knew of the anatomy of his urinary organs and functions. He knew of the existence of kidney, bladder, penis, but had no idea of sphincters and of voluntary and involuntary muscles. I described the function of these organs to him and he followed my words with close attention. When I finished and his face showed that he had understood my words, I asked him whether he had ever actually wet himself during the day.

Charles was taken aback and, with a very surprised look on his face, he shook his head and muttered "no". Very gently I smiled and my hands, in typical Jewish manner, indicated my "so?" He was blown over. He clearly could not find the words to express his sense of discovery and reassurance.

We had to stop our meeting and when they came for a follow-up interview two weeks later, I was told that Charles had not wet his bed or felt the urge to run to the toilet a single time since our session. We now discussed Charles' and his parents' feelings about this turn of events. And what justified the inclusion of this case in this chapter was Charles' phrase when we were discussing the years of trouble they had experienced together. Speaking about their complying to Charles' requests at all times, whatever the circumstances, Mr and Mrs C came to explain their attitude as being entirely based on their love for their son. To their surprise (and mine!) Charles literally exploded: "If a child goes about the house scribbling on the walls, you would expect the parents to teach the child that that kind of behaviour is not acceptable!"

This case is a remarkable illustration of the vicious circle that can be established when the parents behave in what they consider a loving, protective manner, while the child interprets their reaction as a confirmation of his anxiety that there is something wrong, abnormal in his body.

Julie

I never met Julie. It was her mother whom I saw for psychotherapy sessions. Mrs J worked in the financial world and Mr J was a lawyer. According to Mrs J, they had a happy marriage—indeed, the normal ups and downs we find in most, if not all, marriages. Julie was five years old and she had a brother, aged three. One day, Mrs J came to see me and she was obviously very proud of being able to tell me "a marvellous story": the family were enjoying a happy Sunday meal when

Julie turned to her father and asked: "Daddy, do you like being boss?" Both parents were shocked and promptly embarked on a passionate lecture on equality. Eventually, they remembered to ask Julie what led her to ask that question. "Because you, Daddy, are older than Mummy!" and after a brief pause, "I'll never marry anyone older than me!"

I agreed with Julie's mother that this was a marvellous example of the logic that a child's mind can follow. Certainly, a sentiment to be enjoyed, rather than something to be corrected.

Michael

This is a different story, since it is not so obvious to know how to interpret the child's words. It was Mrs M who came to see me for therapy. One day, she was telling me about her six-year-old-son, Michael, and I found myself commenting that I had the impression he was afraid that someone might be dying on him. Mrs M agreed with me and told me that her maternal grandmother was now seventy-eight years old. The day before our session Michael had told her that he would never get married. Mrs M asked him why he said this. Michael said: "Great Granny said she wants to be at my wedding". And Mrs M went on to tell me how she had interpreted her son's words: "I think Michael is afraid that his Great Granny might die *if* he did get married". I could not stop putting forward my interpretation of Michael's words: I thought he was afraid that she might die and then he would find it impossible to get married.

And what is *your* interpretation?

Javier

I was asked to see this six-year-old Spanish boy because he kept messing himself and occasionally also bed-wetting. The family had just migrated to England and Javier had only acquired a minimal amount of English words. My knowledge of Spanish helps me to "get around", but there is a limit to my knowledge of the language. It was a colleague who was familiar with my work with children who believed I might help Javier and referred the family to me.

Mrs J brought Javier to the consultation. A senior financial officer, she "stepped back" to let Javier speak to me while concentrating on her tablet. The boy quickly made himself at home and seemed well able to make sense of my "Portuñol" (Portuguese + Spanish). He told me of his school and home life—always successful back in Spain, he now felt a bit anxious about his capacity to learn English and make friends. Predictably, we got to the point of discussing his sphincter problems and we managed to communicate reasonably well, but the point was reached when I could not express effectively my wanting to know of his emotional experience over his problems. I tried several phrasings, but Javier looked puzzled and eventually looked to his mother.

And Mrs J just managed to move away from the tablet and said in a firm, almost impatient and irritated voice: "El te pregunta como te sientes cuando te cagas!"—meaning: "He wants to know how you feel when you shit yourself!" I was horrified at the crudity (cruelty?) of her words and tried to find a polite way to tell Mrs J that this was a hurtful choice of words. But I had to return to Javier's problems and I tried my best to find words that might help Javier. I told Mrs J of the importance of teaching Javier a routine to open his bowels and to emphasize that all tests had shown he had no physical abnormality.

Sadly, however, I didn't believe any of my words would ever be followed. And I feared Mrs J never even imagined that change was possible—or that it mattered to her how her son felt about his problem.

I did offer them a follow-up appointment, but Mrs J said she would contact me if she wanted to consult me again. Not surprisingly, I heard no further from her.

Claude

This was a thirty-two-year-old French comedian who had been living in London for several years. An immensely complex family history must have influenced his experience of life, and he came to see me after consulting quite a number of physicians and psychiatrists, who had, unfortunately, not managed to provide him with any effective therapy. He suffered from migraines and depression, and had been struggling with his relationships. A number of girlfriends had been part of his life, much as innumerable one-night stands that led to repeated failures and frustrations. However, he published comedy books and made successful appearances in various media.

Why am I presenting him here? One day he gave me the painful, precious statement: "When I say that I've had enough and want to kill myself, people laugh, thinking this is my being funny ..."

Claude's story confirms the validity of a Brazilian saying: "cria fama e deita-te na cama" ("once you establish a reputation, you can lie down: it will carry you").

Sarah

This was a charming lady in her mid-thirties who came to see me because she wanted help to reach a decision regarding an intimate relationship she was involved in. She had succeeded in her professional career, in spite of an incapacitating beginning of life. She was born deaf and she was already over three years old before the parents discovered this was the case. Somehow, she had learnt to lip-read and communicate with people, so that the parents only suspected the presence of a problem when they finally noticed that Sarah did not respond when they spoke to her from behind. She had years of speech therapy and went on to obtain senior university degrees. She eventually obtained a job, working in a very important company as a specialist in "human resources". I thought this was an impressive list of achievements and proof of resourcefulness, but in our meeting, Sarah summed up her problems with these words: "I can help people with their problems, but not myself with mine …"

I did voice my surprise and disbelief at Sarah's view of herself and I urged her to engage in therapy, but she was reluctant to pursue this. I felt that however successful she had been when overcoming her difficulties, she might have remained afraid that even if able to "overcome problems", she had never achieved "full normality" of her personality structure.

Juan

I was asked to see Juan when he was five years old. His parents had been worried about his developmental milestones for most of his life and had now decided to seek a diagnostic evaluation and appropriate treatment. After a long diagnostic interview I was convinced that he had an inborn abnormality that might not be totally corrected and I recommended a thorough psychological assessment and, ideally, long-term therapeutic help.

A geographical curiosity might be of interest. Mr J came from one of the Southern countries of Spanish-speaking South America, while Mrs J came from the Northern countries of South America. When I asked how had Mr J's parents reacted to his choice of partner, Mrs J exploded: a true nightmare! She had never been accepted, always treated as an outsider! Interestingly, when Juan made a drawing of his family, he placed his mother well away from the other members of the family …

Juan had problems with walking and speaking. Toilet training was a nightmare and they had consulted many specialists—for years Juan would defecate anywhere and smear his faeces all over the place with his hands. Only recently had this been overcome and had become "normal". But now Juan refused to speak Spanish …

Both Mr and Mrs J occupied senior positions in their careers. They had travelled in many countries and were now living in London. A younger daughter presented no problems at all.

I found Juan incredibly articulate and amazingly bright. He spoke without any difficulties and made some drawings, again feeling very comfortable when explaining and discussing what he had drawn. He told me about his multiple fears: light, dark, surprises, pain. But I am describing him here because of a fascinating sentence he voiced: "When I get a scary thought, I know that if I can cut it out, it's a daydream—but if I continue seeing it, then it's a dream".

Though I did not see Juan and his parents again, I know that the family found an analyst near their home, who took Juan on for individual sessions and requested a through psychological assessment of his personality. Unfortunately, however, I have not learnt of their findings.

Freddy

This boy's story is described in more details in Chapter Four "Interesting stories", but he voiced a point of view which I felt deserved to be quoted in this present chapter. Freddy suffered from nightmares and it emerged in our interview that his father watched horror movies every night—and allowed Freddy to sit with him. Considering Freddy's descriptions of his dreams, I came to make the comment that he was afraid of death. And to my amazement, he corrected me: *"It's not death I'm frightened of, but of dying!"*. I was really struck by this sentence!

Kay

This bright and articulate six-year-old was referred because her behaviour at school was provoking great antagonism from her teachers.

Seen with mother and stepfather, we could discuss her development and the various family relationships that might be relevant to an understanding of her problems at school. Kay's father had left the family when she was only two years old and her mother had brought up Kay and her sister (two years older) on her own until she formed a relationship with the man she later married. Kay's mother was well aware of her daughter's intelligence and she took great pride in the girl's capacity to express herself, though this might well be one of the factors that made Kay's life at school rather difficult.

Kay's stepfather told me many times of how impressive was Kay's brightness but he was aware of his struggle to cope with her in their daily life. He was not particularly articulate and his whole life led him to expect children to comply with what adults considered right. Predictably, he found himself oscillating between indulging Kay and, at times, enjoying her "lip" and then resenting her capacity to tie him up in knots: at which point he would become the strict disciplinarian, demanding obedience and silence. When I saw them, Kay and her parents could talk about the difficulties of getting Kay to comply with expectations without an argument about the issue under discussion.

Kay's mother tried to obtain some explanation from Kay about her attitude to her stepfather. Eventually, she asked Kay "Don't you like him?" and Kay answered: "Yes, I do, I like him a lot, but I don't love him". Her mother was very surprised by this: like her husband, she saw no difference between the two words. "Why not?" and Kay "I like him, but I don't want to love him and then he will go away".

I was thrilled to hear this reply and I could not understand why both mother and stepfather reacted to Kay's answer as no more than one further proof of her capacity to talk her way out of any attitude that was expected of her. They turned to me and insisted that I should recognise how crafty she was in avoiding any kind of compliance with what they saw as normal child behaviour. I explained to them how rare it was for a child of six to express such insight into her feelings: I stressed how painful and fearful her experiences of life must have been (considering her father's leaving the family when she was only two years old) if she dreads being abandoned by those she loves, and I tried to convey that if such a view of life is not uncommon, it is seldom that we find someone aware of the nature of this anxiety and even rarer to have someone articulating it so clearly. Kay's stepfather was rather dubious about my explanation, but her mother smiled and soon moved nearer to Kay, joining her in the game she was playing, now clearly proud of her daughter and, hopefully, also conscious of her capacity to support and comfort Kay.

Mrs Brown

This is a rather common example of what we call "family life", though as time has moved on, it has become quite uncommon that we should find families living such close lives. But this is a case I met many years ago and I have always cherished recollecting it. Mrs Brown was in her late forties and so was Mr Brown. They had two children who were now in their early twenties. Parents were leading very active, successful professional jobs. Son, twenty-two, was at University away from London and daughter, twenty, had a job placement also out of London.

Because Mrs Brown resented her husband's "coldness", they had attempted marital therapy that they found unhelpful, and Mr Brown had embarked on individual therapy. Mrs Brown was given my name by a colleague of mine and came to see me a few times. Each session was taken over by her bitter, frustrated accounts of how Mr Brown treated her and how each child would call her every single day—at least once!—to relate, complain of the problems they were experiencing. However she never resented being called, she would always respond to their pleas. "This is what is called family life!" she said and I could not stop myself from smiling. "You know", she added, "I do the same to my mother—when I can't cope any more, I call her and tell her of my aches and pains! That's how family life goes, it's important because then I feel better from letting it off my chest!"

I could not resist the temptation and I told her an old story. The husband was racing around the flat, totally defeated and ashamed because he had no money to pay the rent to the flat owner, who lived above their flat. Eventually, the wife got hold of a broom and knocked it several times on the ceiling until the owner shouted: "What's this?" and the wife shouted back "my husband has no money to pay you the rent tomorrow!" and, turning to the husband: "You can relax—he is now the one who feels frustrated and unable to go to sleep!"

Joanna

This lady brought her six-year-old son for a consultation. He suffered from encopresis and kept messing himself, not only day and night at home, but sometimes also at school. After a few interviews and resorting to several incentives the boy did manage to learn how to control his bowels. This case is described here because of two interesting findings. One was the boy's response when asked what he would like to receive as a reward for his success: he asked for money. Not only I, but also his parents were surprised with this choice. "I prefer to get myself something with the money, rather than having to accept what they choose to give me", he explained. The other surprise in this case was Joanna's answer when I enquired about the way in which each parent dealt with his/her bowel functioning. "Oh, my husband? You can set the time on your watch when you see him going to the loo!"

The challenging question in this case was what role the father's defecating routine had played on the toilet training of their son. I would hypothesize that Joanna was reluctant to see her son developing the same obsession regarding his sphincter functions and, if this was the case, I would presume that our discussions enabled her to change her approach to the son and, eventually, "allow" him to learn that it was in his power to control his sphincter, that is, believe he was normal.

Giles and Harry

These boys were twelve and ten years old when they came to see me. Giles was finding it difficult to cope with school and homework and the school psychologist suggested they consulted me. He was very close to his younger brother Harry and they were continuously clashing physically and verbally. For some unknown reason, Harry was taller and more physically developed than Giles and this gave him an advantage when fighting Giles—and yet, most strikingly, Giles would always find excuses and defend his brother whenever their parents tried to intervene.

I saw the boys and the parents a few times and the "chemistry" between the boys improved to some extent. The reason they are being quoted is because of exchanges that happened when I was talking to them. Giles told me of a situation that occurred rather often. When Harry made some mistake in his Maths homework and their mother pointed this out to him, Harry would burst out, shouting abuse at her. Giles was frantically trying to explain WHY Harry shouted at mother, even when in full knowledge that he was wrong. I asked Giles if he knew the expression "shooting the messenger"? No, he didn't know it, but … "perhaps it is that if you are given a bad message, you don't think of what is wrong, you only react to the person who is giving you the message?" Even if correct, he was not happy with his words and went on trying to find better ones. I tried to help him, putting it in different words: "mother is saying 'sum is wrong', but Harry hears 'how can you be such an idiot?'" Both jumped, bursting out in loud laughter: "that is exactly what it is!" And Giles added "I had not thought of looking at it like that" and after a brief pause, he found it important to point out to me that there was no real hostility in Harrys' behaviour, "it is an automatic reaction with him …"

The parents of these boys had grown up in very traumatic circumstances and the family had to cope with frequent crises. Giles was more intelligent and articulate than his younger brother, but from an early age he had presented complex problems in his social relationships and this had led to clashes with teachers and colleagues. For his part, Harry was not so intellectually gifted, but he was much better able to socialise. From an academic point of view, it would be quite challenging to determine the relevance of the parental input to the development of these brothers with such different personalities.

Melanie

This is an example of the powerful effects produced by a person's self-image. Melanie was in her late sixties when she was referred to me. Depression, insomnia, anxiety, feeding problems, relationship difficulties—there was no end of pain and discomfort. Melanie was married to a retired lawyer and had two sons who had successful marital and professional lives. Melanie was a distinguished academic, having conducted elaborate research in her field, publishing many books and articles. But personally, in herself, there was little *joie de vivre*.

Melanie had gone through a number of surgical interventions for orthopaedic and gynaecological illnesses. But telling me about these, the crucial, repeated complaint was the dismissive, cold, not interested manner in which she had always been treated by all specialists and nurses. At the time she came to see me, she was being investigated and treated for intense muscular pain that made it difficult for her to move around. Describing these consultations Melanie said that the doctor "*probably wished I stopped seeing him*". Indeed, she confirmed that this is what she feels about everyone in her world. However much she wishes to improve and lead an active life, she keeps meeting challenges and obstacles that repeatedly expose her to these painful encounters with professionals.

After a brief pause, Melanie said with a very diplomatic, apologetic tone of voice that she was afraid she was boring me—I had been very silent and she had just seen me closing my eyes. I took her words as an unusual compliment: she was trusting me enough to question how I was reacting to her accounts. I managed to smile and told her about Groucho Marx's famous sentence: "I don't want to be a member of a club that wants me for a member". She knew the phrase, but she did not know how I interpreted it: if someone wants me, then it means that they don't really know me—that is, the way I feel about myself, nobody in their good sense would ever want to have anything to do with me.

Melanie managed to smile. "That's true … I do feel something like that … Sorry …"

Frederic

It was many years ago that I saw this twenty-one-year-old young man for a diagnostic consultation. He told me of his complex family history and of multiple experiences of failures in social, academic, and work life. In mid-adolescence he had a breakdown and was admitted to a psychiatric hospital for several weeks. He had been given many different medications, with varying results. Haloperidol was one of these drugs and, after taking it for a while, he stopped it: "What is the point? It only disguises the self from the self!"

We discussed how to proceed and I urged him to have individual psychotherapy. I did not have a vacancy at that time and I gave him the names of a couple of colleagues. Frederic said he would contact one of them, but I did not get any further information from him.

Shirley

This thirteen-year-old girl was incredibly articulate and insightful, but this did not stop her from facing difficult problems at school and in her social life. Her parents had struggled through innumerable conflicts and eventually agreed to divorce. Shirley lived with her mother and kept close contact with her father. Her mother had urged her to see me and Shirley did not mind coming to see me, but she made it quite clear that she had no intention of having therapy at that point in her life.

Discussing her relationship with the parents, she said: "My father tells people what he believes I think—we were called to my school and he told the teachers various stories, always stressing that these were my thoughts and feelings—and I had to control myself not to correct him. My mother does ask me questions and I do answer her, but she only hears what she wants to hear".

Shirley gave me another gem in collating words when I urged her to see a psychotherapist and asked her whether she would prefer to see a man or a woman: "It makes no difference—it could be Father Christmas and I would still be saying the same things".

I felt sad and guilty because of my failure to convince Shirley to have therapy. In spite of her striking command of language and her level of intelligence, Shirley was not a happy young adolescent. She refused my offer of a new appointment and I did not have further news about her progress. I can only hope that she did change her mind and agreed to consult a professional.

Louise

The GP of this charming seven-year-old girl referred her to me, hoping I might help her with sphincter problems she was not managing to overcome. Louise's mother brought her to our consultations and, however loving, protecting, and devoted she was, Mrs L struggled with body disturbances caused by MS and this influenced her views about body functioning and medication—and the intervention of doctors … We had a few meetings and Louise seemed to improve her body control. Louise would often wet herself and when I asked her how did she explain that such lack of control did not affect her bowel functions, she gave me the answer that led me to quote her here: "oh, because wee is liquid and stools are thicker!" And I had another gem as the discussion progressed. Louise was getting tired and a bit impatient with my questions. I had asked her to make a drawing of her body and, when I focused on the way in which she had depicted her pelvis, she realised that I was trying to "convince" her that she had no organic, anatomical abnormality and she interrupted me: "I know there is nothing wrong with me! If there was something wrong, I would be wetting myself all the time!"

I urged Mrs L to convince Louise to have regular psychotherapy to help her overcome her unconscious identification with her mother, but unfortunately my notes do not clarify whether she did embark on therapy.

Mum's hug

Here is an expression that I found quite irresistibly poignant. A lady came to see me because of marital problems. As I always do, I was asking her about her earlier experiences and also about her other social and family relationships. She gave me quite a complex family history, where both father and mother were seen as extremely brittle persons. She was one of four siblings and I was told a painful history where love was indisputable, but the oscillations between closeness and distance were simply unpredictable. But my patient happened to have a close relationship with one of her sisters. Throughout their lives they always shared their feelings about friends, colleagues, and family. And it was when focusing on this last chapter that I was told this unique formulation, aiming to portrait the image of emotional "closeness" in their family: "from time to time, my sister and I exchange a mother-hug: patting each other's shoulders with outstretched arms …"

Suzana

This lady was already in her late fifties when she decided to request a consultation. One of her friends had given her my name and our meeting left me feeling sad that, after a long life and many attempts at therapy, there was little chance that I would really succeed in bringing some happiness to Suzana's life. She did come for a few meetings, but then decided to travel abroad and I had no further news.

Suzana's parents occupied important positions in society, but they were immensely disturbed people. They could provide physical comfort to their two children, but no more. Unfortunately, from a young age, Suzana had developed a severe form of asthma and this had plagued her all her life, occasionally requiring hospital admission.

I am including this story here because when she was in her early teens, Suzana was taken to see Dr Donald Winnicott. She loved the meeting, but suddenly became horrified and sad when, having finished their squiggle game, Winnicott grabbed all the sheets of paper, crumpled them up and just threw them on the floor. "I was hurt, I thought he was going to keep them and look at them later!" she said to me. But the main point of this story is that when Suzana's father was brought into the room, Winnicott, quite sharply told him "this girl needs no analysis! What she needs is a father who is present!"

Johan

This gentleman came to see me because he was struggling with a great number of problems in both his family and professional life. Now in his sixties, he could look back and recount an impressive list of successful enterprises in several business ventures and in the language field. He spoke several languages, he had taught some of these and he had published books and written theatre plays.

Johan accepted my recommendation of having long-term psychotherapy and I later heard from the colleague to whom I had referred him that Johan was less depressed and managing to sort out his problems.

The reason I am including him in this chapter was an expression that Johan used during our consultation: "All my life I have found myself telling me that 'you escaped, but you won't be free'". Clearly living with an inescapable death sentence.

Note

1. Charles' case is also published in Brafman, A. H. (2016). *The Language of Distress: Understanding a Child's Behaviour*, (pp. 23–27). London: Karnac.

CHAPTER SEVEN

Students' stories

Source

I was fortunate to be invited by Dr Peter Shoenberg, on behalf of the Winnicott Trust, to run supervision seminars for the medical students attending his psychotherapy department at University College Hospital. These were enjoyable and rewarding years: the students were not "required" to attend my meetings and this meant that I worked with students who were keen to enlarge their knowledge. This work brought my way problems that I had only met many decades earlier when working in an in-patient unit of a general hospital.

Siblings' love

This student reported seeing a twenty-three-year-old young lady who had been admitted to hospital because of being depressed and possibly suicidal. Two years earlier, her sister who was two years older than her had died. This young woman had always threatened to commit suicide and their mother was always terrified that she might actually do so. One day the sister phoned their mother and, as she happened to be busy, said she would call again later. No calls came and as the sister did not answer the phone when the mother phoned her the next day, the mother went to the girl's flat and discovered her dead in the bathtub: post-mortem investigation showed that she most probably had had an epileptic fit when lying in the bath, hitting her head on the tub. Predictably, the mother blamed herself for this tragedy.

The student asked the patient whether she had ever felt suicidal. "Oh, no," she answered. "My mother always says that if I ever killed myself she and father would be devastated." But, as their conversation went on, the young woman admitted that when she was fifteen, she had one day taken a large amount of iron tablets—and later discovered that this had taken place at the same time that her sister was taking an overdose.

The patient said that all their lives she and her sister had been very competitive. She told our student what high, very high marks she had obtained in her exams, but added: "What is the point? I cannot really go to the cemetery and tell my sister about this …"

I heard a similar story from a patient of mine. An old lady who was a relative of my patient had lost her husband and this left her feeling very "empty" and, time and again, she would say: "What is the point of having something good? There is no husband to share it with …"

Getting in touch with the patient[1]

One day, a young woman discussed a twenty-four-year-old man who had been referred to the psychiatric department because of a severe depression. He had come to Britain from an African country when a revolution led to the break-up of his family: his father had been killed, some of his siblings had gone to America, others had stayed behind with their mother and he was the only one who came here. In spite of having lived in London for some eight years, his English was still quite poor.

The patient told the clerking student that he had had abdominal problems all his life, but various treatments had kept him going. About one year ago, however, he had severe rectal bleeding and was taken to a casualty department. He was admitted for further investigations and Crohn's disease was eventually diagnosed. He was discharged after about one week, but only a fortnight later he had to be readmitted and he had now been in the same surgical ward for the last nine months.

The student had not read the patient's notes and she could only recount what little information the attending nurses had given her. The patient had had part of his bowel removed and he was being fed through a gastric tube, which was due to be removed a few days later. She did not know why he had other tubes going into the right side of his upper abdomen and the patient could not explain the reason for this, either. The surgical team had requested the psychiatric consultation because of the patient's intense depression, which had not responded to any amount of explanations or reassurances.

As the group of students discussed the case, various suggestions were put forward: the patient might be afraid of the further course of his illness, he might be feeling lonely and missing his family, he might be wishing for an end to his pains and, who knows, he might be wishing he was dead. I asked the students to try and find words that would describe the *experience* of the patient when in such a painful and uncertain situation. The young woman who had clerked him came to suggest that perhaps he felt "he had lost part of himself". After further discussion, I said that she was quite probably right, but I suggested that a more accurate description might be that he had lost a part of "*his self*", that is, he could no longer recognise the continuity between his *present* situation and what he had learnt was his *self* in the past.

Some students could not agree to my formulation, but the young woman decided to go back to the patient. Instead of the cold, detached, depressed man she found earlier, she was surprised to see that he received her with a warm, welcoming smile. She apologised for not having stayed with him long enough earlier on and asked him if he had perhaps thought of other things he might want to tell her. She described his response as "if (she) had opened a Pandora's box". His eyes filled up with tears and he told her of his experiences throughout the crisis that had broken up his family and the world he had known. He had witnessed murder, rape, plundering, arson, fights with all kinds of weapons, blood letting in most disturbing ways—and he had been forced to face all this only too aware of his helplessness and his total incapacity to offer support or comfort to those around him.

This was a most sensitive and gifted young medical student. Her knowledge of psychodynamics was nil and her experience of psychotherapy non-existent. But her heart could recognise what was happening and this helped her to find the words to say to the young patient: he had lost family and country and he had now lost part of his body as well.

The patient now burst out crying and, contrary to British mores, but true to his background, he moved his hands and held the student's hands. She accepted this, trying hard not to cry herself.

I had my own reward: when the student contacted me to describe her experience and to thank me, she phrased this in a precious way: I had helped her to discover what happens if you give your patient the chance to put into words what *really* afflicts him.

It is important to add that the patient's depression improved after the students visit. His Crohn's disease will continue to require treatment and, in view of his response to the student, he would be offered the opportunity of further one-to-one psychotherapy.

Depression

At another meeting with the UCH students, one of them described her interview with an in-patient admitted to the psychiatric ward. As happens very often in these situations, the student appeared to be focusing less on the patient himself, than on her interaction with the Senior Registrar and, eventually, the Consultant. She could not make full sense of the comments these two had made when discussing the patient's diagnosis. Apparently, the Consultant disagreed with the Senior Registrar's diagnosis and they had embarked on a sophisticated discussion of symptoms and diagnoses. After a while, a similar discussion developed among the students in my group. But my surprise—and the reason for this account—was the unexpected explosion of one of the students. She had, obviously, been trying to control herself and behave like a "proper" good student. She said: "I *can't* understand this! Depression, bi-polar, depressive syndrome: all my life, I have met people who were unhappy, fed up, sad, furious, disheartened, agitated, exhausted, drained—no end of similar labels! And now we are supposed to go for the 'correct' diagnosis—depression! Depression! Doesn't really make sense!"

The ensuing discussion was simply fascinating. It was obvious that every single student agreed with this young woman's views, but still quite a few of them tried very hard to follow what they believed was a "proper medical appraisal" of the clinical situation. The point was reached when they turned to me: what did I think? I smiled and said that all of them were right: it is the context of a discussion that determines what language is used.

I could not refrain from telling them a classical Jewish story. A couple facing serious clashes came to consult a Rabbi. Seeing the wife on her own, the Rabbi kept nodding and muttering "you are right, my daughter, you are right ..." When he met the husband, again he went on saying "you are right, you are right, my son". Indeed, both husband and wife left feeling comforted and supported. But then the Rabbi's student who had watched this meeting turned to the Rabbi and said: "Rabbi, forgive me—but you said the wife was right, then you said the husband was right—surely, they cannot both be right!" The Rabbi squeezed his beard, moved the head sideways and eventually said, "My son, you are also right ..."

In other words, seeing me in a supervision, discussion meeting, ordinary, colloquial language was perfectly correct—but when a consultant performs his role as teacher of a discipline, he cannot but focus on the evaluation of signs and symptoms that would justify a proper diagnosis of the patient's condition.

A very rude patient

The students described a ward round in which they had seen "a rude and uncooperative lady". The moment the group of students got to her bed, she snapped: "who are all these people?" The Consultant explained they were medical students. But the patient pointed to the Senior House Officer and said: "She is a bitch! Always that stupid grin on her face!" The patient suffered from disseminated lupus erythematosus and had apparently suffered some strokes that had provoked muscular disabilities.

The students knew that the patient refused to be discharged because her mother did not want to have her back living with her. Furthermore, only by certification had the doctors managed to have her admitted, since she was showing such impossible behaviour.

After a while I asked about the patient's age: twenty-four. "Did this matter?" I asked. "No" they answered. I was surprised, since I had expected some sign of sympathy for another young person going through such a dramatic health crisis. In view of their cold "no", I reminded them of the saying "there, but for the grace of God, go I". This appeared to shock them—they seemed to think about this and their faces showed a friendlier expression. One of the students now decided to mention that a member of staff had also commented that the Senior

House Officer in question smiled too much. Perhaps this was a result of embarrassment, but it still bothered many people. After some more discussion, they mentioned that the patient was black. I smiled—does this make a difference? The students made faces, indicating doubts, puzzlement. I decided not to voice my belief that staff and other patients might be more sympathetic to the patient if she was white.

What I did put to the students was my impression that the patient's "hostility, loss of control" might result from an underlying feeling of despair and hopelessness. Considering the students' positive reaction to my comments, I told them of my conviction that a doctor can only learn of his patient's true feelings if he asks them the right question—but sadly only a rare doctor will decide to invest his time in "opening the gates" and listening to his patient's accounts.

Mothers and babies

Source

During their first year, all students accepted for training at the British Psychoanalytic Society have to carry out weekly visits to mothers who have just given birth to their babies. Ideally, one hopes that their reports will throw light on how they have processed their own life experiences. Considering that the majority of students are well into their thirties, one presumes that their family and social lives will have influenced how they see this mother–baby duo learning to live with each other. But reality does not totally confirm such assumptions. Running these "Baby observation" seminars, time and time again, I found that many students seemed to put aside their own life experiences and, instead, to "read" the mother/baby interaction as evidence, proof positive, of what they were learning about theoretical psychoanalytic schools in their personal training analyses.

Breast-feeding

One example was a student reporting that the mother she was observing complained bitterly about her three-week-old baby "biting her breast". The student had no doubt that here was evidence of "oral sadism", a baby acting on his inborn sadistic instincts and attacking the mother's breast. The other two students attending this seminar discussed this interpretation. They both knew the presenting student was in a Kleinian analysis and was, accordingly, finding confirmation of Melanie Klein's theories. One of the students chose to follow Winnicott's theories agreeing with the "attack on the breast", but this coming from the baby testing out mother's love and capacity to survive the baby's hostility.

Fortunately, life does play unexpected tricks on us and whenever we can extend our observations we have the opportunity of learning about further developments. When the student visited that mother the following week, she found a smiling, delighted, proud mother thoroughly enjoying breast-feeding her baby. And now? How does one explain such a dramatic change? Simple! That week the mother had been visited by a breast-feeding counsellor and learned how to present her nipple to the baby.

The reporting student was a lady in her early forties and she did smile when reporting that week's visit. But did this change her devotion to Klein's theories on early development? Of course, not …

Mothering

A student described how a seven-month-old baby was playing in the playpen and suddenly fell sideways. He began to cry and look around, anxiously, for his mother. Without delay, the mother did walk to the playpen, a broad, warm smile on her face, making gentle, comforting, loving sounds and words to the baby. As she stretched her arms and lifted up the baby, he stopped the crying and soon was displaying a sweet smile, clearly reassured, feeling safe again.

Turning to another student in the group, I asked him how would a similar situation unfold with the mother–baby couple he had been observing. He burst out laughing; "Oh, God! No way! If my baby fell like that and cried, the mother would come running, virtually crying herself and lift the baby, embracing her, murmuring words of love and comfort, as if dealing with a seriously wounded baby!"

The first student was clearly taken aback. "Of course", he said, "mothers are different from each other and so are babies, but it is always amazing to discover how true this is!"

I took the opportunity to mention an important consequence of these observations: from the moment that the carer panics, it becomes impossible to ascertain whether the baby is reacting to the surprise of his fall, to any presence of pain *or* to the carer's panic.

Pathological?

Here is the text of the report written by an analytic student who was observing a baby, now six-and-half months old:

"The mother went to get us cups of tea, while I observed A. He seemed focused either on the toy or the mirror, it was hard to tell. He had small, nearly pinpoint pupils:- light blue irises and his attention seemed fixed. He was making small movements and changing expressions, smiling then looking puzzled, then smiling again, generally seeming absorbed and involved, contented although active. I watched for several minutes and then tried to see whether he would notice me. It was strikingly hard to catch his attention although I came quite close, smiled and said his name".

This student was a qualified medical doctor. Not just his words, but also the tone of his voice suggested that something of the baby's behaviour had worried him, so I asked him what he had in mind. He hesitated and said: "It felt abnormal … this mother is intrusive, I think the baby is fending her off by concentrating in his own world … and, therefore, also fending me off".

I asked him whether this "fending off and concentrating in his own world" was perhaps an indication that he believed that this was a case of autism. He hesitated, but reluctantly admitted that he had thought this baby might be autistic. He continued to read his notes: "He steadfastly ignored her, continuing to be fascinated by the mirror or toy" … "The mother's repeated 'tell me a story' felt intrusive to me".

We had another two students in this meeting and both of them agreed with their colleague. They all considered the mother insensitive and intrusive—and in-line with prevailing psychoanalytic theories of autism, they felt that this kind of mothering was the cause of the baby's "shutting himself off from the world". It happens that I still remembered the original report of the student's first meeting with the mother, just after the baby had been born and I reminded my students of how relieved and proud she was after having this baby, since she had proved unable to conceive and had gone through many IVFs before finally succeeding in giving birth to this child. I put it to them that I believed that her "intrusiveness" resulted from her anxiety that this baby might also die. No, they could not agree with me …

Fortunately, the following months' visits to this couple led the students to recognise that this was an absolutely normally developing young baby.

Familiarity?

A senior analyst, qualified abroad and now doing the child analysis training at the British Society, came to my seminars for analysts doing this training. He was married to a lady who had adolescent children from a previous marriage. After a few meetings, I was struck by his questions and comments on the children being presented. I could not detect any underlying feelings that might be reflected in his contributions. These appeared "correct", acceptable, relevant, and yet there was a type of coolness, detachment that I felt would never allow me to guess how he would react to the behaviour of the child under discussion. I found myself wondering why he was doing the child analytic training, except because of some intellectual desire to complement his studies, his professional identity.

After a few weeks, I plucked up the courage to ask him if he had children of his own—no, was the answer. And did he have siblings? Friends whose children he had played with? No, the child he was now seeing as part of his training was the first child he had ever come close to … I could only comment on how interesting but difficult he must be finding this new experience.

Note

1. "Getting in touch with the patient" is taken from "Memorizing *vs* understanding", first published in 2003 in *Psychoanalytic Psychotherapy, 17*(2): 119–137, and also in Brafman, A. H. (2010). *Fostering Independence* (pp. 150–151). London: Karnac.

CHAPTER EIGHT

Intra-vaginal non-ejaculating

Object choice

What leads someone to move closer to a particular person they meet and suddenly develop emotions that make him see that individual as a friend and at times to find these feelings becoming stronger and deeper so that they seek to establish a closer, more intimate relationship with him/her?

Psychoanalytic theory considers this "choice of object" as a derivative from that person's early relationship with his parents. Conceivably it is this pattern of choice of a friend or partner where the adolescent or adult moves closer to a person who resembles or duplicates that individual's biological parents, that led to our well known saying that "the apple never falls far from the apple tree", or putting it more accurately, the apple will always seek to find the way back to its tree.

Considering an individual's personality, I believe that his constitutional endowment is just as important as his experiences from birth. His experiences in late childhood, adolescence, and adult life will also influence that individual's experience of himself in the world as well as how he perceives the people around him—in spite of this, when we focus on the individual's choice of a partner or close friend, we usually find that he/she has chosen a person who presents features of that individual's parents.

This formulation of my guiding theoretical framework will not surprise anyone reading the stories in this book. I am making these explicit in this chapter as an explanation, a justification for the cases to follow. Other chapters have described many cases of patients with sexual problems, but in the course of my work I was surprised to notice an unexpected common feature in the histories of men who reported not being able to ejaculate when having penetrative intercourse: they all described their mothers as dominating, inconsiderate, dictatorial, hurtful, intrusive—the adjectives varied, but the resulting images were very similar. They had all tried to move away from their mothers, only to describe how, time and again, they found partners who reproduced many of the features of their mother's personality.

Seeing these men in the consulting room was quite a challenge and, unfortunately, I only managed to help some of them for brief periods of time. I would come up with various interpretations and, presumably, some of these led to an intellectual "insight", but not to a definite change of the underlying unconscious anxieties—or of their presenting complaint.

Nathan

This thirty-five-year-old engineer came to see me, hoping to understand why all his relationships ended in a traumatic fashion. His parents had divorced when he was thirteen years old. He thought his father was "great", but his mother was "stupid, useless—I hated her!"

Nathan had a senior position in his job, but all through his twenties work was a challenge. Time and again he would be offered work, achieve promotions and, suddenly, disenchantment set in and he dropped out. He would spend some time travelling and then another job would be found. His relationships followed a similar pattern: he found a woman who was happy to live together with him, but after a time the relationship would break up.

Throughout his late adolescence and adult life Nathan would find himself experimenting some drink or drug and soon this would develop into an addiction. Nathan sought various sources of help and when he came to see me, he claimed that he was free of alcohol and drug addictions.

It was only in our second or third session that Nathan managed to tell me about his sexual life. He would find a prostitute, with whom he would spend several hours playing out grotesque fantasies that involved humiliation and hitting each other. He would seldom get an erection and when some of these women tried to masturbate him, he had no interest and no reaction.

One day Nathan told me of a meeting with his brother. He showed Nathan some photos from their childhood. They discussed how both had found those years very painful and he reminded Nathan of their mother's obsession with punishing him, invariably sending him away from the table, accusing him of various misdemeanours. It happened all the time that the mother would accuse Nathan of doing something wrong and proceed to hit him. Nathan was struggling with an impulse not to cry when telling me these memories. He went on to focus on his preoccupation in differentiating between being treated unfairly and being humiliated. These were aspects of the fantasies that haunted him most hours of the day. It was at the point where he could not cope with the intensity of these fantasies that he would seek a prostitute.

Nathan had been living together with a partner for nearly five years. They had met when both worked in the same company and a wide circle of friends and colleagues would probably describe them as a happy couple. However, serious conflicts developed between them over the two to three years before our session, since Nathan "lost interest in sex" and his partner felt he never found time to spend with her.

Nathan could not make sense of the fact that even when having sex with his partner he would find himself turning to the fantasies of being humiliated. He could develop an erection when they engaged in sex, but then he would find that he was unable to ejaculate—and his partner saw this as an act of rejection, which was an additional pain to his feelings of helplessness.

Because of his job, Nathan would often have periods of time away from London and, eventually he stopped our sessions. He claimed to value these, but I was left with a sense of failure. I had not managed to help Nathan to change his feelings about women: unconsciously, he always expected them to "accuse" him of not meeting their expectations: clearly, a reproduction of that image of his mother he so much hated.

Roger

This was a remarkably articulate man in his late thirties. Time and again I was impressed with his capacity to convey his experience of being in the world. He seemed to have had a serious emotional crisis in his mid-adolescence. In later years his versatility and obvious high potential led him to repeated successes that would soon be followed by disappointment.

Roger was homosexual and had no conflicts about this. One day he told me: "I felt that the life of a middle-class professional, married with a family was closed to me." As we discussed his daily life, he said: "Walking into a new place, I feel a challenge to make myself wanted." Soon afterwards, he was telling me about his sexual life and made a comment that I was convinced covered not only sexual, but any kind of social encounter: "But I have never allowed anyone to penetrate me, it would be the end, like becoming part of someone else." He told me a memory: he was three years old and he "was alone in a room, not unhappy, there was light and space". He valued being on his own. Roger was aware of the significance of this sequence of valuing being alone, then seeking company and needing to feel wanted, only to escape back to solitude as soon as he found himself accepted or wanted—dreading to be taken over.

Roger lived with his parents until he was thirty years old. "I was dependent on my mother, but also frightened of her … she would repeatedly pounce on me, not physically, just verbally." His parents lived on the continent and, as it happened, his mother was severely ill at the time Roger was seeing me. But, however concerned he was about her condition, Roger spent most of his sessions discussing his social relationships. When telling me of the sexual side of his life, he said: "I have to tell you that I am virtually unable to ejaculate. I have lost many relationships because of this."

Roger told me of his pleasure when imagining or watching men's bodies, particularly their penises.

By contrast, when he was with a sexual partner, if this other man held, wanted to suck Roger's penis or spoke of being penetrated, he immediately lost his erection. He had no end of examples of the effect that closeness to another person produced in him. And, rather sadly, one day Roger told me of an occasion when he was in a gym and another man said: "If I ask you any question, I can virtually see you withdrawing!" This reminded him of his brother saying to him: "it is difficult to understand how whenever I say something to you I can see the shutters coming down!"

A very interesting point emerged when Roger was telling me of his sensation of still being the same person as he was when aged eighteen. As he had used, in passing, the word "mature", I asked him if "to be mature" meant to him being married and having children. He smiled and said: "Yes, yes, in bold, capitals, underlined, in red glowing letters!"

Roger said: "My mother would say 'you must stand up for yourself!' My father would counter this by saying 'no man can be an island'." I said that his tone of voice suggested that his father spoke warmly, in contrast to his mother's aggressive style. "Oh, indeed! Mother was an angry person! I was afraid of her! But I was very fond of my father ..."

Shortly after these sessions Roger was offered a job in another country and stopped his therapy. He seemed to feel that our work together had been helpful, even if he had not achieved any dramatic changes in his style of life. And again I was left wondering if it was possible to affect the unconscious link between having an intrusive, demanding, critical mother and the incapacity to ejaculate.

Charles

This gentleman was in his late forties when he came to see me. He had been married twice and had engaged in several long-term affairs. Like the other men in this chapter, he was unable to ejaculate and only for a couple of weeks after some months of therapy did he find himself ejaculating when with a particular lady-friend.

Charles' father was described as very violent towards his wife and children. He always tried hard to influence the children to follow careers of his choice. Charles' mother was frail and had suffered several psychiatric breakdowns. The first one occurred soon after Charles' birth and it meant that the boy had to be placed with relatives for several weeks. Another serious breakdown occurred when Charles was sitting for his "O" levels and he remembered how difficult he found to reconcile his need to study and the need to visit his mother in hospital.

Contrary, however, to the mothers of the other men described in this chapter, Charles' mother was not violent, controlling, demanding or intrusive. But I am including Charles in this specific pattern of mother/ child relationship because these same characteristics developed with every woman he ever got involved with. With one of them, after failing to ejaculate, he said quietly, passionately "I want you to possess me!" With each of the women with whom he got involved he would engage in physical fights and every one of them was described as volatile, fragile, tearful but also possessive, dominating, aggressive, and violent.

Considering the features of his relationships with women, I cannot avoid the assumption that, in spite of his conscious image of his mother, Charles experienced these women as reproductions of some unconscious image he had of his mother.

Solomon

I have described my consultations with this gentleman in Chapter One "Sex and love". He had managed to find a wife and, previously, other women who were willing to accept his incapacity to ejaculate if having penetrative sex. He would succeed in making these women reach orgasm and they would proceed to masturbate him and help him to ejaculate.

Solomon is included in this chapter because he described his mother as "a dictator". He had several siblings and the oldest sister still lived with their mother, and two of the others were getting older, but quite incapable of forming solid relationships—he smiled and agreed with my comment that perhaps they did not want to risk inflicting on children the life they had been through.

Phillip

This thirty-six-year-old Italian gentleman came to see me in an attempt to understand why he was unable to form any lasting relationship with a woman. Sooner or later he would feel that she wanted to control and dominate him and this promptly led him to bring the relationship to an end, even if quite often he would continue to maintain a friendship with that woman.

His parents were, supposedly a happy couple, both successful professionals who lived in Italy. Phillip had a younger sister who also lived in Italy; she was happily married and had a child. Phillip had moved to England in his early twenties, after qualifying as a lawyer. In England he had a series of different jobs and when I met him, he was a senior IT officer in a large bank.

Phillip had an active social life and he seemed to experience no difficulties with friends and colleagues, in fact they all appeared to value his company and his hospitality. When, however, he focused on describing his relationship with women, he told me that often he was unable to have an erection and, most of the times when he managed to get an erection and penetrate his partner's vagina, he would be unable to ejaculate.

In the course of our sessions, Phillip told me of his childhood and adolescence. In many respects, one would consider his development as perfectly normal, but he also recounted puzzling experiences, even if he had always seen them as no more than ordinary, common life events. He "discovered" he had a penis that would grow in size when he was nine to ten years old, but he never touched his penis and only in late adolescence was he able to actually masturbate. He was in his mid-twenties when he first had a girlfriend and just as with subsequent girlfriends, he soon discovered the problems described above. From the sexual point of view, all these ladies had, apparently, been prepared to accept his problems but after varying lengths of time, Phillip felt that these women wanted to run his life—and this would bring the relationship to an end.

One of my problems, as the analyst, was to discover what attitudes these women were showing that led Phillip to feel threatened. I was struck by an interesting detail in Phillip's accounts: he was able to articulate his experience of having a woman trying to control him, but he would never raise this complaint or accusation directly with the lady in question; instead, he would tell me of deciding to pull back so as not to find himself upsetting, hurting the woman. It took quite a few sessions before Phillip recognised and admitted that "hurting" was, not only an emotional event, but, potentially, also a physical danger. He was clearly very shaken when he finally told me of an occasion many years earlier, when a woman he was going out with had managed to upset him to such a degree that he had punched the wall near her head.

I could not avoid wondering about Phillip's relationship with his mother. This topic started with his telling me that he exchanged email messages with his mother at least once every day. One day he told me that when he, inadvertently, mentioned the name and nationality of a woman he had met, his mother promptly voiced her pessimism about women from that country and urged him not to get too involved with her. Phillip told me that very often his mother would tell him of women she had met in her social circle and that she would make a point of introducing to him when he next visited her.

After several months of therapy, Phillip became involved with a woman with whom he did manage to have successful penetrative sex. But as the weeks went by, it became clear that the lady wanted to establish a closer, deeper relationship—and Phillip promptly found a way of bringing an end to the affair. He could recognise a definite turning point when a woman "took on" the dominating aspects that duplicated his original relationship to his mother. Time went on and Phillip found a woman who often came to London as part of her work and they would spend many evenings enjoying their sexual lives. How would one explain this change? The answer: he was convinced that this woman was perfectly happy with this well-defined, limited contact: she seemed to have no intention of formalising their relationship. Clearly, Phillip was convinced that marriage was the stepping stone at which he would be taken over and lose his independence.

CHAPTER NINE

Music as a language

Disturbed young man

Back in the 1970s I was seeing in psychotherapy a very disturbed young man. He was in his early twenties, experiencing dramatic mood swings and finding it virtually impossible to sustain friendships. He came to a session one day in a highly manic state. A frozen smile on his face, he sat on his chair and kept staring at me, silent. I asked him a question and, taking a deep breath, he started to sing one of the songs of the Beatles. When he stopped, I asked another question and his reply, after a brief pause, was again the lyrics of another Beatles' song. These were not random choices, since the words he sang expressed precisely the answers he meant to convey. This went on for fifty minutes and when I brought the session to a close, he simply got up and left the room.

Thinking as a psychiatrist, I was worried by his condition, but I was also impressed by his meticulous knowledge of the lyrics he so appropriately chose. These were songs that all young people sang at all times in those days, but my patient had turned to them as if they were his own language.

Over the years, I came to recognise that some people do experience feelings that they would not manage to express in their normal articulate language. Having grown up in a family where three languages were continuously used, I had learnt of how certain sentiments are expressed in one language much more precisely than in any other one. Anna Freud and Melanie Klein discovered and described in the 1920s how children can use toys to convey their feelings. My consulting room work showed me how some people, mostly children and adolescents, will indeed use drawings to convey feelings that they would not know to articulate. The patient mentioned above showed me that music can serve the same purpose, that is, an alternative language.

Woman musician

A woman in her early thirties came to see me. A professional musician, besides playing her instrument, she also composed pieces for TV and films. She had decided to consult me because of problems in her marriage: her husband refused to have sex, and it happened that sometimes she might wake up in the night to find that he was masturbating. Worse still, if she voiced her dismay, he would burst out crying and accuse her of unfairly causing him pain. I thought that the most puzzling question here was the reason that led/enabled her to continue in this marriage. Asking her why, how did she manage to continue in this frustrating relationship could only lead to a: "I don't really know …" or the classical "well … I still love him …" I thought about the possibility that these traumatic situations were replicating earlier experiences—she told me she had no memories of similar events. Considering her profession, I decided to suggest she should "play back" the painful sequence of discovering the husband masturbating and that she should stop at the point where he started to cry. In other words, as if this moment was a single, isolated image. When her face showed she had managed to do this, I told her to compose, to form a musical chord in her mind. When her facial expression indicated she had done this, I asked her whether this chord brought back any memories. After a few seconds, she burst out crying. She explained that she "had been there" many times in her childhood. Whenever she dared to tell her mother how unhappy her mother was making her, her mother would burst out crying and accuse her of being an ungrateful, unloving daughter.

Perhaps any psychoanalyst might have suggested to this lady that her present-day experiences were touching some soft wound from her childhood, but I have no doubt that this theoretical formulation would never carry the same power as this lady making the discovery, the connection herself—thanks to resorting to her musical language, she could make the link that ordinary spoken language had not led her to make.

George

I knew that *George* (mentioned in Chapter Three "Unusual stories") had studied and played the piano throughout his adolescence and young adult life. As an adult, the piano was his favourite hobby. In one of our sessions, he came to mention that however active and competent he was in his professional life, he found it very difficult to cope with loneliness. He was aware of his restlessness, but he had trouble to identify what emotions he was struggling with. I thought this was a puzzling formulation, not quite understanding what alternatives he was referring to. I decided to ask him how he managed to identify that emotion. His reply? "I discovered that I can find the answer by paying attention to what piece I had come to be playing on the piano ..."

Hector

I saw *Hector* for an assessment required by his health insurers. He was in his early thirties, a successful IT manager. At one point he told me that he was seven years old when he discovered the world of music. He had piano lessons and then discovered panpipes. It happened that his father was more "traditional" and demanded he learnt to play the transverse flute. Hector acquiesced and played this during his college studies. But as he reached adulthood, he reverted to his beloved panpipes, which he could "play for hours".

As our interview progressed, I asked him if he felt he was "depressed". He replied "what does that mean?" He was not being sarcastic or challenging, so I thought of repeating my question in other words: "what music do you tend to play?" Now Hector smiled: "Melancholic tunes ... mainly Doina, traditional folk music that is played on panpipes". He was quite aware of the link between emotions and choice of music.

After Hector left, I turned to our helpful Wikipedia: The **Doina** (Romanian pronunciation: ['dojna]) is a Romanian musical tune style, possibly with Middle Eastern roots, customary in Romanian peasant music, as well as in Lăutărească. It was also adopted into Klezmer music.

CHAPTER TEN

The replacement child

A middle-aged young man came to see me for a consultation. He was worried and puzzled by the fact that throughout his adult life he kept resigning from jobs he had struggled to obtain. Well, I thought, he was probably one of those people I had come to consider "quitters". However, as he went on to describe these situations in more detail, I recognised that he was not seeking "novelty", adventure—rather, he was reacting to an underlying unconscious feeling that the new position represented a triumph he did not deserve to enjoy—what one might describe as an experience of "non-entitlement". Finding this definition brought to mind a sense of familiarity: I had met other patients who fell into this category. If "quitters" elicited in me a degree of irritation, those patients that I diagnosed as struggling with an unconscious feeling of *non-entitlement* made me feel a degree of sympathy and pity—plus a sense of failure and helplessness that I had experienced when trying to help such patients in the past.

Patients with this unconscious sense of non-entitlement will report repeated experiences of social, educational, and professional endeavours where their efforts led to acceptance, praise, and probable promotion, only to be abandoned for a variety of reasons. Predictably, some patients were aware of this kind of self-frustration and went on to formulate possible reasons that might explain their decisions. One patient said he could not feel proud of his achievement, since he had not worked hard enough to achieve that particular success. Another patient dismissed the significance of the triumph by stressing how much more still needed to be done.

I consulted my clinical notes and, much to my surprise, I found that these cases had a common denominator: their mothers had lost a child or suffered a miscarriage before giving birth to the patient in question. Through this unexpected route, I had found my way to what psychological texts describe as "the replacement child". Most of my patients, however, had never known that their mother had lost a child. It was my identifying the feeling of non-entitlement and raising such a possibility that led them to consult their mothers about the occurrence of such an event.

It was in 1964 that Albert and Barbara Cain[1] published their paper describing "The Replacement Child". They studied six couples that had given birth to a child with the deliberate intention of having a replacement for a child who had died. Many of these parents presented psychiatric pathology and many of the new children required psychiatric help. Cain and Cain's paper gives a detailed account of the innumerable routines that most of these couples developed as reminders of the lost child. They also described the overprotective, distorted, pathogenic way in which these mothers cared for the new, replacement child.

Each of these routines of "keeping the child alive" could not but influence the development of the replacement child and of the older siblings. The very fact that these parents had been referred to Cain and Cain is evidence of the psychiatric problems they were struggling with.

In 1988, Sabbadini[2] described the analysis of two patients brought up as a replacement for a dead sibling and he presented a thorough and fascinating survey of the literature on this theme. He transcribes an eloquent autobiographical testimonial from Salvador Dali (see below) and a description of Vincent van Gogh's ordeal (that can be found in Humberto Nagera's book—*Vincent Van Gogh—A Psychological Study*[3]: both artists grew up struggling with traumatic feelings resulting from having been conceived as replacements for a lost child.

> I lived through my death before living my life. At the age of seven my brother died of meningitis, three years before I was born. This shook my mother to the very depths of her being. This brother's precociousness, his genius, his grace, his handsomeness were to her

> so many delights; his disappearance was a terrible shock. She was never to get over it. My parents' despair was assuaged only by my own birth, but their misfortune still penetrated every cell of their bodies. And within my mother's womb, I could already feel their angst. My foetus swam in an infernal placenta. Their anxiety never left me … I deeply experienced the persistence of [my brother's] presence as both a trauma—a kind of alienation of affections—and a sense of being outdone. (Salvador Dali, Confessions, 1973, p. 12)

The following cases are examples of patients I have seen who presented the syndrome of a replacement child and struggled with this deep, unconscious feeling of *non-entitlement*.

Antoine

This was a PhD student in her late twenties who complained about an unusual problem: she was always late for any appointment. When expected to fulfil a task, time and again she would think about it and invariably decide that there was still time to perform it; she insisted she never failed to present a paper or report on time, but all the relevant work could only be undertaken on the evening preceding the final deadline. Antoine thought this was something she had learnt from her mother: as a child, attending primary school, every day she would have to wait for her mother, who was "every single day" late to come to pick her up.

All her life, Antoine had been praised by her teachers who were always impressed by the high quality of her work. When she did gymnastics and later ballet lessons, again she would be praised. Friends and colleagues also thought very highly of her. And yet she never relaxed, every single engagement gave rise to fear and anxiety. When finished, she never managed to feel pride; it was more a sense of relief, soon followed by dread, anticipating the report of faults and the appearance of the next challenge to be overcome.

After a few months of our psychotherapy sessions, I ended up asking Antoine whether, besides her younger brother, her mother had had any other pregnancies. I explained my question by pointing out the paradoxical reaction she had to every single achievement, as if she was not truly "allowed" to relish her triumph. Antoine said she had no idea about this. But when she next met her mother, Antoine decided to ask her about my comment. Her mother "was frozen", shocked and surprised: before Antoine's birth, she had in fact had a miscarriage.

I continued to see Antoine in therapy. However much she valued our sessions and claimed these were an important factor in her managing her daily life, there was no major change in her sense of self-confidence. Her academic achievements were most impressive, but the feeling of pride continued to elude her. I saw this as a feeling of non-entitlement, a persistent sense of achieving something she did not deserve to obtain.

Nora

It was a colleague who told me this story. A friend invited her to have a meal, so that he could get some help over a particularly painful experience. He had an older sister who had presented very severe emotional problems since her adolescence—now in her thirties, she had never managed to stick to a career or a job, still leading a lonely, depressed life—and a younger brother who was married and looked after his family quite happily. The friend himself was a successful engineer who enjoyed his family and his work. But his mother had been very ill and was finally put under morphine to alleviate her final pain and help her to die. And it happened that when he went over to visit her, his mother struggled to speak and said she was very happy to have all her four children with her. He thought this was an effect of her mental state, but when he mentioned this to an aunt, his mother's sister, she answered, carefully choosing her words, that as a matter of fact, his mother's first pregnancy had led to a miscarriage—and apparently the gynaecologist urged her to have another pregnancy—from which his older sister was born.

I have no details about the emotional problems that this gentleman's sister was struggling with, but I thought I should still describe this story.

Georgia

Born in South Africa, Georgia was eighteen years old when I saw her. She had two older siblings, aged twenty-four and twenty-two, and a younger sister aged sixteen. The family moved to England when Mr G was assigned on a four years contract to a branch of his bank in London. Georgia had a very successful academic life and her applications to Universities in England, USA, and South Africa had all led to an offer of a place. But she was feeling very depressed, unable to fall asleep and crying often at all hours.

Her family life was very complex. Her parents had split up when she was a young child and her mother had embarked on a stormy relationship with another man. Eventually she managed to leave this man and, to everybody's surprise, Mr G came back to live with the whole family.

Georgia came to see me with both parents. When I was seeing Mr and Mrs G on their own, I asked about the "gap" in the children's ages and Mr G explained that after the first two were born, his wife wanted more children, but he was reluctant to accept this. He eventually did agree, but Mrs G went on to have a miscarriage. Both Mr and Mrs G agreed that Georgia was "a special" child, clearly her mother's favourite.

When I saw Georgia on her own, she could hardly stop crying. She was aware of her privileged position in the family and in society, having all her applications to University accepted—but what did she want to do? She said that ideally she would immediately return to her beloved South Africa. As we discussed this, I voiced to her my impression that I thought the precise country did not matter—as long as she could get away from her mother. She was clearly shocked, obviously gratified with my understanding her feelings. She finally managed to find the words to express her feelings: "she wants me to *be* her life!"

Contrary to other "replacement children", Georgia was aware of feeling "not entitled" to enjoy her own, private life. However, it is important to note that she did not seem to feel that she owed her existence to "having taken the place" of a child of a previous pregnancy. Instead, she recognised being treated by her mother in a special way, as if having a specific type of importance to her—and Georgia resented her mother's expectations and demands because of seeing her as a "special" child.

Georgia did manage to go back to South Africa and I have no follow-up on her progress. I hope she was able to seek the help of a psychoanalyst who might enable her to find and develop her sense of independence and self-sufficiency.

Sabine

This was an unexpected finding when checking my files: a variation on my usual definition of a "replacement child". Sabine, then aged fifteen, and her parents came to see me because they were struggling with problems without managing to find a satisfactory solution. Mr S was in his mid-forties and had been placed in London by an international banking firm. He was in his early thirties when he got married. He described himself as very timid, incapable of defending himself—until he discovered the world of psychoanalysis, which, he said, had helped him enormously. His sister had always been a source of trouble in the family, but they got on reasonably well, even though living in different countries. Mrs S was in her early forties. She described her mother as a "dominating general". She had always worked as a journalist and when she gave birth to Sabine, she left work. She spoke in an agitated manner and described herself as brittle, often having temper explosions.

Sabine had always been a brilliant student, but totally obsessed with full success: not knowing the answer to a single question was enough to throw her into painful despair. Mrs S found it necessary to emphasise that they (the parents) had never put any pressure on Sabine. They could not understand why their daughter was so unhappy most of the time. She had life-long friends and many colleagues at school, and yet she behaved as if she was not able to meet their expectations. Her teachers always praised her work, but homework and tests were painful tortures, Sabine dreading failure.

When I saw Sabine on her own, she gave me a detailed account of her failed relationships. The typical pattern was some disappointment leading to total withdrawal. To my surprise, she said that the only person to whom she would react and enter into a fight was her mother. Sabine told me of a dream she had when eleven years old: someone had been murdered and she woke up in a panic, staying awake for hours.

In another session Sabine told me of her preference to "come second place". She suspected that perhaps coming first would expose her to envy. Because her favourite subject was mathematics, I suggested that considering –5 and +5, she preferred to stay at zero, to avoid comparisons and competitions. She smiled, agreeing with me. She now moved on to speak about her wider family: she only maintained contact with her father's family. Her paternal grandmother had died when Sabine was four years old and "because (I) was the only girl among the grandchildren, (I) had always been her favourite."

I had thought in previous sessions that because of being an only child, perhaps Sabine was a replacement child, but I was unable to find enough evidence for this. But suddenly Sabine told me that since she was born the family said she was "exactly the same as her paternal grandmother—the skin, facial features, body shape". What she could remember but could not understand was the fact that after his wife died, when the grandfather first met Sabine (then four years old), he embraced her, kissed her, and could not stop crying.

I do believe that this experience of "replacing grandmother" may well have been the basis for her later incapacity to feel entitled to enjoy her success. Further sessions did help Sabine to feel less anxious, but she stopped our sessions when her father was transferred to another country.

Carole

It was several decades ago that I saw this unhappy twenty-two-year-old young woman. Carole consulted a gynaecologist colleague of mine because of not having had periods for many months. My colleague found an extremely thin young woman who had already been diagnosed as anorexic and had several ineffectual admissions to hospital. Having established that there were no hormonal abnormalities, she told Carole that she should see me for a consultation.

Carole was clearly an intelligent and articulate young lady, but extraordinarily thin and anxious. She told me of a traumatic situation: a friend invited her to go on a rowing boat trip and she refused, feeling caught up with her eating anxieties. It happened that something went wrong and her friend's boat capsized and he died. Carole felt terribly guilty and was now dreading any involvement with friends. She spent most of her days having tests following applications for modelling: she was invariably rejected because of being "too thin". She told me of her father shouting and demanding she should have a proper meal—"he should know by now that my dinner is half a little bar of chocolate …" We spoke about her views of men and sex. Carole told me that she was not interested in sex and, surprisingly, she pointed out that in practice she feels there is a link between eating and sexuality, which gives her a further reason not to eat, that is, to prevent the possible appearance of sexual feelings.

I next saw Carole together with her parents. Her mother was very short and overweight. Carole had described her as "overpowering, outspoken, pushy". She was composed in our interview and told me of her frustration that such a capable daughter should not allow herself to study and develop a profession. Carole had described her father as strict, forever criticising her for her choice of friends and for her staying out of the house, while now he went on demanding she should go out, "do something". In our meeting, Mr C was mostly quiet, giving me the impression that he did not believe he could help Carole.

When I next saw Carole, much as at our first meeting, she spoke of her fear of death and dying. "I think about it all the time". I asked her if this was because of her friend's death, but she didn't really believe that was the only reason. She had a definite feeling that she was not "living to the full", which sometimes led her to wish for a positive resolution, while most of the time it only led her to wish for dying.

Now that I have described Carole's experience of life, I would like to quote her mother's telling me that, though Carole was their only daughter, she had in fact gone through six miscarriages. I was completely surprised and looked at Carole, who told me that she remembers the last miscarriage happening when she was six years old, though she cannot recall how she registered it.

It was extremely difficult to find mutually convenient times for further sessions, but I saw Carole for a few more meetings. She said the sessions were helpful and she was managing to implement some changes in her life. A couple of years after we stopped, I had a request from Mr C to write a referral of Carole to one of the NHS psychotherapy clinics.

Central question: considering Carole's awareness of her struggles to avoid the fulfilment of potentials, desires, wishes, how significant are the miscarriages? I do believe this stems from a feeling of non-entitlement, a sense of guilt for being the only survivor of all her mother's pregnancies. Unfortunately, this was another case where I did not manage to help the patient to achieve a sense of entitlement to benefit from her potential gifts.

Gerald

This thirty-year-old man had been consulting a colleague for over two years and now felt that some important issues were not being resolved—having decided to see a new therapist he was given three names and I happened to be one of these. He was a very successful humorist, but he struggled with feelings of depression and dissatisfaction, never managing to celebrate a triumph, often reacting with guilt and anger when praised. He told me of his past and present life. He had learnt when quite young that his mother had been born and lived in Germany before managing to escape the Nazi anti-Semitic persecution. One of her sisters had also come to the UK, but when he asked mother about another sister, she replied: "you will have to ask Mr Hitler". He was puzzled when seeing my reaction to this answer: I had found it a surprising touch of black humour.

But this Holocaust experience was only one of several experiences that led Gerald to the awareness of death. The illness and eventual death of a grandfather had been a very important event in his childhood and he did remember asking his mother (when he was seven years old) what was death. She answered: "it is a kind of falling asleep from which you never wake up". And Gerald was quite convinced that this had led to his being an insomniac for most of his life.

Focusing on his relationship to his parents, Gerald told me that when he was eighteen years old, he learnt that his mother had had an abortion before he was born: apparently, she did not want a child and had fallen pregnant even though wearing a cap. He turned to his sense of humour and said: "This child must have come from a strong sperm!" We went on with our discussion and I could not avoid making it explicit how preoccupied he was with life and death—he agreed with me and I ventured posing the question, "And what if your mother had not had an abortion?" and Gerald answered immediately: "Oh! I would not have been born!"

Gerald had become accustomed to "paying the price" for being a renowned comedian. He was the person who gave me one of the most poignant renderings of the difference between how one feels and how one is seen by the world. "If I happen to say that I am feeling depressed, people burst out laughing, thinking that I'm joking …"

Gerald contacted me a few days later to thank me for our meeting, but he had decided to have his therapy with a female colleague of mine.

Notes

1. See Cain, A., & Cain, B. (1964). The replacement child. *Journal of the American Academy of Child and Adolescent Psychiatry, 3*: 443–456.
2. See Sabatini, A. (1988). The replacement child. *Contemporary Psychoanalysis, 24*: 528–547.
3. Nagera, H. (1990). *Vincent Van Gogh—A Psychological Study*. International Universities Press.

INDEX

For Product Safety Concerns and Information please contact our EU representative GPSR@taylorandfrancis.com Taylor & Francis Verlag GmbH, Kaufingerstraße 24, 80331 München, Germany